CCNA GUIDE TO
Cisco Networking
Fundamentals
Lab Manual

Kelly Cannon,
CCNA, CCAI

COURSE
TECHNOLOGY

Thomson Learning™

ONE MAIN STREET, CAMBRIDGE, MA 02142

Australia • Canada • Denmark • Japan • Mexico • New Zealand • Philippines
Puerto Rico • Singapore • South Africa • Spain • United Kingdom • United States

CCNA Guide to Cisco Networking Fundamentals Lab Manual is published by Course Technology.

Associate Publisher	Kristen Duerr
Senior Acquisitions Editor	Stephen Solomon
Product Manager/Developmental Editor	David George
Production Editor	Jennifer Goguen
Quality Assurance Tester	Neil Malek, CCNA
Associate Product Manager	Laura Hildebrand
Marketing Manager	Susan Ogar
Text Designer	GEX Publishing Services
Composition House	GEX Publishing Services
Cover Designer	Efrat Reis

Disclaimer

Course Technology reserves the right to revise this publication and make changes from time to time in its content without notice.

The Web addresses in this book are subject to change from time to time as necessary without notice.

For more information, contact Course Technology, One Main Street, Cambridge, MA 02142; or find us on the World Wide Web at www.course.com.

For permission to use material from this text or product, contact us by

- Web: *www.thomsonrights.com*
- Phone: 1–800–730–2214
- Fax: 1–800–730–2215

ISBN 0-619-00091-0

Printed in Canada

4 5 6 7 8 9 WC 02 01

TABLE OF CONTENTS

CCNA GUIDE TO CISCO NETWORKING
FUNDAMENTALS LAB MANUAL

INTRODUCTION

This lab manual is designed to be used in conjunction with the first edition of *CCNA Guide to Networking Fundamentals* by Hudson and Cannon. Inside this manual you will discover over 40 hands–on lab exercises designed to increase your understanding of the networking concepts presented in the above text as well as in the first half of the Cisco Networking Academies curriculum.

While it is possible to obtain CCNA certification status without hands–on experience, it is almost impossible to successfully interview with a prospective employer without citing specific experience. This lab manual fills in the gap left by traditional textbooks that focus on concepts but do not provide opportunities to gain in–depth hands–on experience.

Most technology–type books provide some hands–on exercises at the end of the chapters that are designed so those students can work through them at their own pace. Conversely, many of the lab exercises in this lab manual require teamwork and instructor participation. The labs are challenging and complex to the point that they were separated from the text and compiled into this manual.

FEATURES

In order to ensure a successful experience for both instructors and students, this book includes the following features:

- Objectives – Every lab has a list of learning objectives
- Materials Required – This lists all of the materials required for the lab
- Activity Sections – The labs are broken down into manageable sections
- Step-by-step instructions
- Questions where appropriate to make sure students are meeting the objectives

HARDWARE REQUIREMENTS

Chapters 10 and 11 of the textbook involve router configuration. Some of the lab exercises refer to the Cisco Networking Academies Semester 2 lab setup. This lab setup is illustrated in Chapter 10 of this lab manual. The Cisco Networking Academies Semester 2 lab setup, as well as many of the lab exercises in this manual, require the following materials:

- Four 2501 series routers with power cables
- One 2514 series router with power cable
- Five hubs with power cables
- Three V.35 DTE cables (male)
- Three V.35 DCE cables (female)
- Six UTP patch cables
- Six Ethernet 10BaseT UTP to AUI transceivers
- Five RJ-45 to RJ-45 rollover cables
- Five RJ-45 to DB-25 or DB-9 connectors
- Power strips
- Five Windows 95/98 computers with the COM2 port available

CHAPTER ONE

INTRODUCING NETWORKS

Labs included in this chapter

➤ Lab 1.1 Install Memory in a Workstation
➤ Lab 1.2 Install a Hard Drive in a Workstation
➤ Lab 1.3 Install a Network Interface Card (NIC) in a Workstation

LAB 1.1 INSTALL MEMORY IN A WORKSTATION

Objective

The objective of this lab is to help you become familiar with hardware installation, specifically memory installation. In this lab you will remove and install SIMMs (single in-line memory modules). Installing memory is the single most frequently performed workstation upgrade, because it is the most cost-effective way to increase workstation performance. After completing this lab you will be able to:

➤ Identify the memory in a workstation.

➤ Use the proper safety technique when working with electronic components.

➤ Remove and install SIMMs.

Materials Required

This lab requires:

➤ One complete workstation for every four students

➤ At least four SIMMs in each workstation

➤ One or more wrist-grounding straps

➤ Small Phillips screwdrivers

ACTIVITY

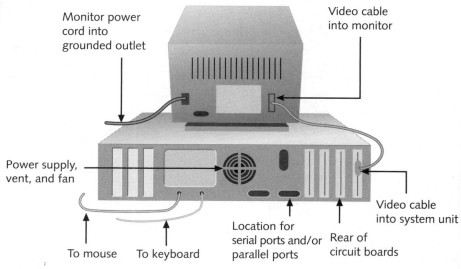

Figure 1-1   Standard workstation configuration

1

1. Observe the configuration of the workstation. Figure 1-1 shows a standard workstation configuration.

2. Identify parallel and serial ports, the network interface card (NIC), the power supply, the video card, and keyboard and mouse ports.

3. Make sure the computer is off. If it isn't, shut it down properly.

4. Disconnect all cables connected to the computer.

5. Unscrew the system unit cover.

6. Put on the wrist-grounding strap. Clip it to a piece of unpainted metal on the system unit.

7. Locate the memory banks on the motherboard.

8. If necessary, unscrew and remove any components blocking access to the SIMMs.

9. Using both thumbs, pull the clips that hold the SIMM in place away from the SIMM. Use your fingers to push the SIMM forward at a 45-degree angle as shown in Figure 1-2.

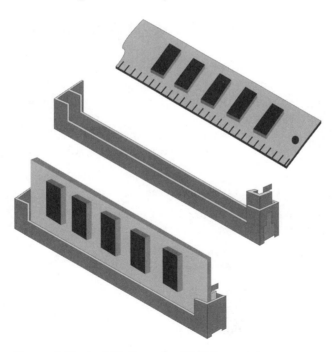

Figure 1-2   Installation of a SIMM

10. Pull out the SIMM by the edges of the modules.

11. Repeat Steps 9 and 10 until you have removed all SIMMs.

12. Now, practice installing the SIMMs. Hold a SIMM at a 45-degree angle over the first available slot. The first slot should be labeled Bank 0.

13. Guide the SIMM into the slot.

14. When the module is aligned properly, snap the module into place, perpendicular to the motherboard. If the module doesn't snap in easily, you may have it facing the wrong way.

15. Repeat Steps 12 through 14 until you all have installed all modules.

16. Screw any removed components back into place.

17. Screw the cover back on the system unit.

18. Reconnect all cables connected to the computer, including the cables for the monitor, mouse, keyboard, and power.

19. Turn on the workstation and enter the CMOS setup program.

20. Verify that the setup program recognizes the memory.

21. Save and reboot the workstation.

LAB 1.2 INSTALL A HARD DRIVE IN A WORKSTATION

Objective

The objective of this lab is to help you become familiar with hardware installation, specifically hard drive installation. In this lab you will remove and install a hard drive. In recent years, hardware requirements have exploded. At the same time, hard drives have become relatively inexpensive. Installing a new hard drive is a commonly performed workstation upgrade. After completing this lab you will be able to:

➤ Identify the hard drive in a workstation.

➤ Use the proper safety technique when working with electronic components.

➤ Remove and install a hard drive.

Materials Required

This lab requires:

➤ One complete workstation for every four students

➤ At least one IDE hard drive in each workstation

➤ One or more wrist-grounding straps

➤ Small Phillips screwdrivers

ACTIVITY

1

1. Observe the configuration of the workstation.

2. Identify parallel and serial ports, the network interface card (NIC), the power supply, the video card, and keyboard and mouse ports.

3. Make sure the computer is off. If it isn't, shut it down properly.

4. Disconnect all cables connected to the computer.

5. Unscrew the system unit cover.

6. Put on the wrist-grounding strap. Clip it to a piece of unpainted metal on the system unit.

7. Locate the hard drive. It may be mounted against the wall of the system unit, or it may be mounted in a bay at the front of the unit.

8. Unplug the IDE cable (ribbon cable) and the power connector from the hard drive. Note that the red edge of the IDE cable should be on the left, next to the power connector.

9. Remove the hard drive by unscrewing it from the system unit.

10. Detach the other end of the IDE cable from the controller card. Note that if the connector on the cable faces away from you and points toward the controller card, the red edge of the cable is on the left, aligned with pin 1.

11. Now, install the hard drive by screwing it back into place.

12. Plug the IDE cable into the hard drive with the red edge of the cable next to the power connection.

13. Plug the power connector into the hard drive.

14. Attach the other end of the IDE cable into the controller card. Line up the red edge of the cable on the left as you are facing the card and aligned with pin 1.

15. Screw the cover back on the system unit.

16. Reconnect all cables connected to the computer, including the cables for the monitor, mouse, keyboard, and power.

17. Turn on the workstation and enter the CMOS set-up program.

18. Verify that the setup program recognizes the hard drive.

19. Save and reboot the workstation.

LAB 1.3 INSTALL A NETWORK INTERFACE CARD (NIC) IN A WORKSTATION

Objective

The objective of this lab is to help you become familiar with hardware installation, specifically NIC installation. In this lab you will install a NIC. Currently, most businesses and some home environments are networked. Every networked PC requires a NIC. Installing a NIC is another commonly performed upgrade. After completing this lab you will be able to:

➤ Identify a proper adapter slot on the computer motherboard for a NIC.

➤ Use the proper safety technique when working with electronic components.

➤ Install a NIC.

Materials Required

This lab requires:

➤ One complete workstation for every four students

➤ A software-configurable NIC for each workstation

➤ At least one available adapter slot for a NIC in each workstation

➤ One or more wrist-grounding straps

➤ Small Phillips screwdrivers

ACTIVITY

1. Observe the configuration of the workstation.

2. Identify parallel and serial ports, the power supply, the video card, and key board and mouse ports.

3. Make sure the computer is off. If it isn't, shut it down properly.

4. Disconnect all cables connected to the computer.

5. Unscrew the system unit cover.

6. Put on the wrist-grounding strap. Clip it to a piece of unpainted metal on the system unit.

7. Locate an available adapter slot that matches the pin configuration of your NIC. Figure 1-3 shows typical configurations. The card and slot type must be the same with one exception. You can place an ISA card into an EISA slot.

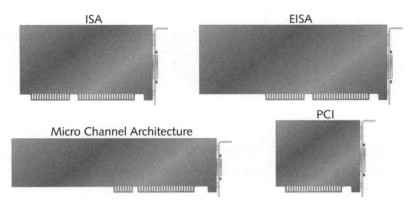

Figure 1-3   Typical pin configuration of a network interface card (NIC)

8. Unscrew and remove the slot placeholder if one is associated with the slot.

9. Hold the card by its upper corners and position the edge of the connector directly over the PC slot.

10. Rock the card back and forth from left to right while you push it firmly down into the slot.

11. Screw the edge of the card down onto the system unit.

12. Screw the cover back on the system unit.

13. Reconnect all cables connected to the computer, including the cables for the monitor, mouse, keyboard, and power.

14. Turn on the workstation and check to see if the computer boots properly. If it doesn't, you may need to shut down and reseat the NIC card.

15. If you are using Windows 95 or Windows 98, Plug and Play may recognize your NIC card and attempt to configure it. Let it try. If it doesn't succeed, continue to Step 16.

16. Click the **Start** button, click **Settings,** then click **Control Panel**.

17. Double-click **Network** then Click the **Add** button.

18. Double-click **Adapter**.

19. Choose your NIC card from the list.

20. Click **Have Disk** and put the diskette with the NIC drivers on it in drive A.

21. If you are using Windows 95 or Windows 98, Plug and Play may take over and finish the installation for you. If it doesn't, continue with the installation procedure as prompted, and then continue with Step 22.

22. Reboot the computer. You will probably be notified if there is an IRQ or I/O conflict. If so, continue to Step 23; otherwise; shut down the computer.

IRQ or I/O Conflict

23. Right-click **My Computer** and choose **Properties**.

24. Click the **Device Manager** tab.

25. Click your **NIC card** and click the **Properties** button.

    If there is an IRQ or I/O conflict, it will be indicated at the bottom of the property sheet.

26. You can change the configuration until you find one that works. You will then have to reconfigure the card to match the Windows settings. You will need the diskette that came with the NIC to do this.

27. Reboot when no IRQ or I/O conflicts are indicated.

28. Shut down the computer.

NETWORK DEVICES

Labs included in this chapter

➤ Lab 2.1 Create and Use a Bootable Diskette

➤ Lab 2.2 Use FDISK to Manage Partitions

➤ Lab 2.3 Format Partitions and Install DOS

➤ Lab 2.4 Make the Hardware Connections Between a Workstation and the Network

➤ Lab 2.5 Create a Diskette to Attach a Workstation to the Network

➤ Lab 2.6 Install Windows 95/98 over the Network and Configure for Network Access

LAB 2.1 CREATE AND USE A BOOTABLE DISKETTE

Objective

The objective of this lab is to teach you to create, use, and understand the purpose of bootable diskettes. There are many reasons why you would want to boot to drive A (presumably your diskette drive) instead of booting to your hard drive. For example, you may not have an operating system on your hard drive yet, or the operating system may have been corrupted. You may want to partition and format your hard drive. Very often, these operations are initiated via a floppy disk. In this lab you will examine and copy the files necessary to create a bootable diskette. You will then boot a workstation with the diskette inserted. After completing this lab you will be able to:

➤ Identify the files required to create a bootable diskette.

➤ Create a bootable diskette.

➤ Boot a workstation to drive A using the bootable diskette.

Materials Required

This lab requires:

➤ One complete workstation for every four students

➤ DOS or Windows 95/98 installed on the workstations

➤ Diskettes

ACTIVITY

1. Boot the workstation and enter the CMOS setup program. There is usually a hot key that you can press that takes you to this setup program. This key normally appears at the bottom of the screen when the machine is first booted.

2. Check to make sure that the workstation is set to boot first from a diskette in drive A and then to the hard drive (C). This is the default for most computers, but you can check by entering setup mode when the computer first boots up. During boot up the screen displays a message such as "Press F1 to enter setup" or "Press Del to enter setup." When you are in setup, you can browse through the menus until you find the order the computer will search for the boot information. Usually, the bottom of the screen displays the keys to navigate and operate this program.

3. Exit the setup program and let the computer boot as normal.

2

4. To create a bootable diskette, you need to copy the COMMAND.COM file from the hard drive to a diskette. In addition, you copy the FDISK.EXE file and the FORMAT.EXE file. These additional files are used when partitioning and formatting the hard drive.

If you are using DOS, complete Steps 5 and 6, proceed to Step 10, and continue through the end of the lab exercise. If you are using Windows 95 or Windows 98, proceed to Step 7 and continue through the end of the lab exercise.

DOS Workstations

5. Put a formatted diskette in drive A.

6. Type the following commands at the C: prompt, pressing **Enter** at the end of each line. Do not type the information in parenthesis.

Sys a: (*This command transfers the operating system (command.com) to drive A.*)

Copy fdisk.exe a:

Copy format.com a:

Windows 95/98 Workstations

7. Put a formatted diskette in drive A.

8. Click **Start**, click **Programs**, then click **MS-DOS Prompt**.

9. Type the following commands at the C:\WINDOWS prompt, pressing **Enter** at the end of each line. Do not type the information in parentheses.

Sys a: (*This command transfers the operating system (command.com) to the A drive.*)

CD command

Copy fdisk.exe a:

Copy format.com a:

10. Put your newly created boot diskette in drive A.

11. Restart your computer properly.

12. Your computer should boot to drive A and you should see the A: prompt.

13. If you get a "Non system disk" error message, the COMMAND.COM file did not transfer or is corrupt. Try recreating your bootable diskette.

14. When you are sure the diskette works, remove it from the drive and restart your computer properly.

LAB 2.2 USE FDISK TO MANAGE PARTITIONS

Objective

A partition is a logical division of a hard drive. The increasingly gigantic hard drives lend themselves to this subdividing. Instead of just having drive C, you can create drive D and so on, using the same hard drive. The active partition is the one the computer will use to boot from. The objective of this lab is to provide you with the ability to use FDISK to manage hard drive partitions. FDISK is the most commonly used partition-managing software. While you can purchase many other programs that do what FDISK does and more, FDISK is free and very quickly lets you view, create, and delete partitions. After completing this lab you will be able to:

➤ Use FDISK to view partition information.

➤ Use FDISK to delete a partition.

➤ Use FDISK to create partitions.

➤ Use FDISK to set the active partition.

Materials Required

This lab requires:

➤ One complete workstation for every four students

➤ DOS or Windows 95/98 installed on the workstations

➤ Bootable diskettes with FDISK.EXE on them

ACTIVITY

1. Boot the computer using a bootable diskette. The diskette should have FDISK.EXE on it.

2. Type **FDISK** and press **Enter** to start the utility.

3. Type **4** and press **Enter** to view the partitions currently on the hard disk.

4. Press **Esc** to return to the main menu.

5. Type **3** and press **Enter** to delete the primary partition.

6. Type **1** and press **Enter** to choose the primary partition.

7. If a volume label is associated with the partition, you must type it. If there is no volume label, just press **Enter**.

8. Confirm the deletion by typing **Y** and pressing **Enter**.

9. Press **Esc** to return to the main menu.

10. Type **4** and press **Enter** to make sure it deleted.

11. Type **1** and press **Enter** to create a new primary DOS partition.

12. Type **N** and press **Enter** when asked if you want to use the maximum available space for your partition.

13. When prompted, type the size in megabytes of the partition you want to create. Create a 50 MB partition by highlighting the default number and typing **50**.

14. Press **Enter** then press **Esc** to return to the main menu.

15. Type **2** and press **Enter** at the main menu to set the active partition.

16. Type **1** to choose the partition you just created, then press **Enter.**

17. Press **Esc** to return to the main menu.

18. On your own, create a 100 MB extended DOS partition.

19. Now create a logical partition out of the total extended DOS partition.

20. Press **Esc** to exit the FDISK utility.

LAB 2.3 FORMAT PARTITIONS AND INSTALL DOS

Objective

The objective of this lab is to teach you to format the partitions you created in Lab 2.2 and to install DOS on drive C. You will use your bootable diskette with the FORMAT.COM command on it. After completing this lab you will be able to:

➤ Use the FORMAT.COM command to format the two partitions on the drive from Lab 2.2.

➤ Use the DIR.EXE command to see directory listings and verify the sizes of the two partitions.

➤ Install DOS on drive C.

Materials Required

This lab requires:

➤ The workstations previously partitioned in Lab 2.2

➤ One workstation for every four students

➤ Bootable diskettes with FORMAT.COM on them

➤ The three DOS setup diskettes

ACTIVITY

1. If necessary, boot the computer using your bootable diskette.

2. Type **FORMAT C:** and press **Enter** to format drive C.

3. Type **Y** and press **Enter** to confirm the format.

4. When prompted for a volume label, type **DOS** and press **Enter.**

5. Type **FORMAT D:** and press **Enter** to format drive D.

6. Type **Y** and press **Enter** to confirm the format.

7. When prompted for a volume label, type **WIN95** and press **Enter.**

8. When the formatting process is complete, take the floppy out of drive A, and replace it with DOS setup diskette #1.

9. Reboot.

10. Follow the directions to install DOS on drive C.

11. After rebooting, ensure you are at the C prompt. If you are not, change to drive C by typing **C:** and pressing **Enter.**

12. Type **DIR** and press **Enter** to see a directory listing. What is the total size of drive C? _____

13. Change to drive D by typing **D:** and pressing **Enter.**

14. Type **DIR** and press **Enter** to see a directory listing. What is the total size of drive D? _____

LAB 2.4 MAKE THE HARDWARE CONNECTIONS BETWEEN A WORKSTATION AND THE NETWORK

Objective

The objective of this lab is to make sure you understand the hardware basics of how to connect computers to the network. In this lab you will connect four computers to a hub using UTP (unshielded twisted-pair) cable and then connect the hub to the telecommunications outlet as shown in Figure 2-1. You will then connect the workstations to each other and to the hub using thinnet cable. Finally you will connect the hub via UTP cable to the telecommunications outlet. After completing this lab you will be able to:

➤ Connect computers to a hub using UTP cable.

➤ Daisy-chain computers together using thinnet cable.

➤ Connect a hub to a telecommunications outlet.

Materials Required

This lab requires:

➤ Four workstations partitioned and formatted with DOS installed from Lab 2.3

➤ NICs installed in the four workstations that support both UTP and thinnet cable

➤ Hub that supports UTP and thinnet connections

➤ Five segments of UTP cables

➤ Five BNC-T connectors

➤ Two 50-ohm terminators

➤ Four segments of thinnet cable

ACTIVITY

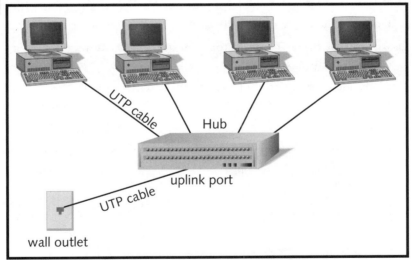

Figure 2-1   Connecting the network using UTP (unshielded twisted-pair) cable

UTP Only

1. If the hub is active, plug it in using its power cord.

2. Connect a segment of UTP cable from the RJ-45 transceiver on a computer NIC to an RJ-45 port on the hub. Make sure you are not using a port on the hub labeled "uplink".

3. Repeat Step 1 for the other three computers.

4. Connect a segment of UTP cable from the RJ-45 port on the hub that is labeled as the "uplink" port or the port marked with an "X" to a telecommunications outlet with an RJ-45 port.

5. How is this uplink port different from the other ports on the hub?

_____

_____

6. What is the alternative to using the uplink port?

_____

_____

7. Disconnect all cables.

UTP and Thinnet

8. If the hub is active, plug it in using its power cord.

9. Connect a segment of thinnet cable to a BNC-T connector.

10. Attach the BNC-T connector to the BNC transceiver on a computer NIC.

11. Connect the other end of the thinnet cable to another BNC-T connector.

12. Attach that BNC-T connector to another BNC transceiver on a computer NIC.

13. Continue daisy-chaining the computers together with the thinnet cable and BNC-T connectors until you have wired together the four computers and the hub as shown in Figure 2-2.

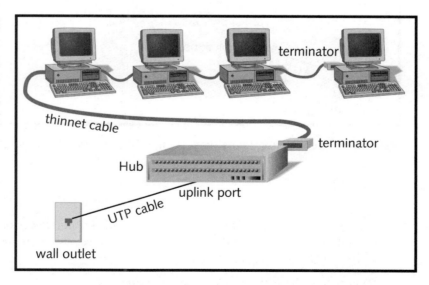

Figure 2-2   Connecting the network using UTP and thinnet cable

14. Both ends of this bus configuration must be terminated. This means you must put a 50-ohm terminator on the BNC-T connector on the last computer in the chain, as well as on the BNC-T connector on the hub.

15. Connect a segment of UTP cable from the RJ-45 port on the hub that is labeled as the "uplink" port or the port marked with an "X" to a telecommunications outlet with an RJ-45 port.

LAB 2.5 CREATE A DISKETTE TO ATTACH A WORKSTATION TO THE NETWORK

Objective

The objective of this lab is to teach you to create a diskette that will connect a workstation to a network server. This is a common method used to access software stored on network file servers and download it to workstations that are not yet network-ready. In this lab you will create a diskette that attaches a workstation to a NetWare file server or an NT server. After completing this lab you will be able to:

➤ Create a diskette that will connect a workstation to a network server.

➤ Use the diskette to attach to the network.

Materials Required

This lab requires:

➤ A Novell NetWare and/or NT server with a shared directory containing the Windows 95/98 installation files

➤ Four workstations partitioned and formatted with DOS installed from Lab 2.3

➤ The workstations connected to the network in Lab 2.4.

➤ Diskettes

ACTIVITY

Novell NetWare Server

1. Boot the DOS workstation. You should boot to the C: prompt.

2. Move to the directory containing the EDIT.COM file. To search all subdirectories for this file, you can type **DIR EDIT.COM /S**.

3. Change to the correct directory using the **CD** *subdirectory* command, where *subdirectory* is the name of the subdirectory that contains the EDIT.COM command.

4. Type **EDIT.COM** and press **Enter** to open the DOS editor.

5. Type the following lines, pressing **Enter** after each line. Do not type the information in parentheses.

Lsl

Smc8000 *(This is just an example. You will need the name of the NIC driver that matches the NIC in your computer.)*

Ipxodi

Netx /ps=lapis *(Lapis is the name of my NetWare server. You must substitute the name of the NetWare server with the shared Windows 95 installation files on it.)*

F:

Login password *(Password will be the password you must supply to access the server.)*

Map g:=data:win95 *(In this example, data is the name of the NetWare volume and win95 is the name of the shared directory with the Windows 95 installation files in it.)*

6. Put a formatted diskette in drive A.

7. To exit and save, hold down **ALT** while you press **F [ALT+F]**. Then press **X**.

8. When you are prompted, press **Y** to confirm the save.

9. Press **ALT+ D** to go to the Directories: box. Scroll down with the down arrow key until you get to drive **A**. Press **Enter** to choose drive A as your destination.

10. Press **ALT+N** to go to the File Name: box.

11. Type the filename **net.exe** and press **Enter**.

12. In addition to the batch file you have just created, you will also need the NIC driver on the diskette. Your instructor will tell you the file's name and location. Substitute that file name for [driver] in Step 13.

13. Move to the directory containing the NIC driver, type the following command, and press **Enter** to copy the driver to the diskette:

Copy [driver] a:

14. Change to drive A, and type **net.exe** then press **Enter**.

15. You should be at the F: prompt, which indicates that you have attached to a NetWare server.

16. Change to drive G. You should be pointing to the shared Win95 directory.

Windows NT Server

1. If you have an NT Server, you can use the Network Client Administrator program to create a network access diskette.

2. Put a bootable diskette into the NT Server drive A. *Bootable* means that the diskette must have the COMMAND.COM file on it. You created a bootable diskette in Lab 2.1.

3. Click **Start**, click **Programs**, click **Administrative Tools**, then click **Network Client Administrator**.

4. Click the option to **Make Network Installation Startup Disk,** then click the **Continue** button.

5. In the Share Network Client Installation Files dialog box, click **Use Existing Path**, then click **OK**.

6. In the Target Workstation Configuration dialog box, click the floppy disk type: **drive A is 3.5"**. Figure 2-3 shows the dialog box.

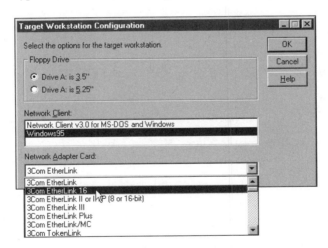

Figure 2-3   Creating a Windows 95 boot disk using Network Client Administrator

7. In the Network Client: box, select **Windows 95.**

8. Use the Network Adapter Card: list box to select the NIC appropriate for the computer from which you will be attaching. Click **OK**.

9. Assume that there are enough Windows 95 licenses for this lab, and click **OK** when warned about the necessary license requirement.

10. Type a computer name in the Network Startup Disk Configuration dialog box. Figure 2-4 shows this dialog box.

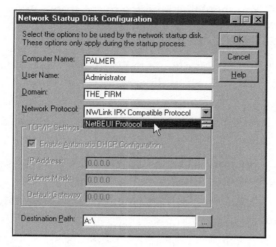

Figure 2-4 Configuring a Windows 95 boot disk using Network Client Administrator

11. You can leave Administrator as the user name,but you will be prompted for the Administrator password when you attempt to connect.Your instructor may wish to assign a different user name and password.

12. Leave the default domain name.

13. Set the protocol to **NetBeui** if you can or to **TCP/IP.**

14. The destination path should be A:. Click **OK**.

15. Click **OK** again to accept the configuration.

16. After the diskette is created, click **OK,** click **Exit** in the Network Client Administrator dialog box, then click **OK** again.

17. Take the diskette out of the server and place it in drive A of the workstation you want to attach.

18. Boot the workstation.

19. You should attach to the shared folder with the Windows 95 installation files on it.

LAB 2.6 INSTALL WINDOWS 95/98 OVER THE NETWORK AND CONFIGURE FOR NETWORK ACCESS

Objective

The objective of this lab is to teach you how to copy Windows 95/98 installation files over the network and how to install and configure Windows 95/98 for network access. In this lab you will install and configure Windows 95/98. After completing this lab you will be able to:

➤ Copy the Windows installation files to the workstation.

➤ Install and configure Windows for network access.

Materials Required

This lab requires:

➤ A Novell NetWare and/or NT Server with a shared directory that contains the Windows 95/98 installation files.

➤ Four workstations partitioned and formatted with DOS installed from Lab 2.3

➤ The workstations connected to the network in Lab 2.4

➤ Network diskettes created in Lab 2.5

ACTIVITY

Novell NetWare Server

1. Attach your workstation to the NetWare server with the diskette you created in Lab 2.5.

2. Change to drive G and type the following command to copy the directory and all files and subdirectories containing the Windows 95 installation files to drive C. Press **Enter** after you type the command.

   Xcopy *.* c:

Windows NT Server

1. Attach your workstation to the NT server with the diskette you created in Lab 2.5.

2. Locate the shared directory on the server. Change to this directory and type the following command to copy the directory and all files and subdirectories containing the Windows 95 installation files to drive C. Press **Enter** after you type the command.

   Xcopy *.* c:

The Install

3. After you copy the directories and files, change to the directory on drive C by typing **CD \directory** (where *directory* is the directory containing the windows setup files), and press **Enter**.

4. Type **Setup** and press **Enter**.

5. If you are using the Upgrade version of Windows 95, you will be prompted to locate a previous version of Windows. Your instructor will give you the first setup diskette from Windows 3.1 or Windows 3.11. Insert the diskette into drive A, click the **Continue** button, then click the **Locate** button. Change to the drive A in the list box, and click **OK**.

6. When prompted to choose a directory for the install, change the C:WINDOWS path to **D:WINDOWS**.

7. At the Setup Options window, click **Custom** install. Do not choose Compact install.

8. When prompted for your name and company, type **Cisco#** for the name (where # is an identification number provided by your instructor for the computer you are using) and type your **school name** for the company.

9. You will be prompted for the CD key code. Your instructor will provide you with this number. Type the code and press **Enter.**

10. When prompted to let Windows 95 analyze your hardware, click **No**. Deselect any devices from the list box if you know your computer doesn't have them.

11. In the Get Connected window, don't select any communications options.

12. In the Select Components window, deselect everything you don't need.

13. In the Network Configuration window, a client, adapter, and protocol will probably be listed. They are there because you have already made a connection to the network. If the TCP/IP protocol is not listed, click the **Add** button, click **Protocol**, click **Microsoft**, then click **TCP/IP**. Click **OK**.

2

14. If the Network Information Required window appears, be prepared to configure the IRQ and I/O range for your network interface card (adapter). Your instructor will give you these numbers. The numbers listed may be the correct ones.

15. In the Computer Settings window, make sure the settings are correct.

16. When prompted to make a Startup Disk, click **No** unless your instructor needs one.

17. The files will begin copying to your D:WINDOWS directory. This may take up to 15 minutes depending on your hardware.

18. At the Finishing Setup window, click the **Finish** button.

19. Remove any diskettes from drive A, as the system will reboot.

20. Since the TCP/IP protocol was added, you may get the message, "DHCP unable to get IP." If you aren't using a DHCP server, click **No**, then click **OK**.

21. Press **ESC** when prompted for a Windows user name and password.

22. In the Regional Settings window, select the correct time zone.

23. Click **Cancel** when prompted to set up a printer.

24. Once again the computer will be rebooted.

25. Press **ESC** when prompted for a Windows user name and password.

Configure for the Network

1. Right-click **Network Neighborhood** and click **Properties**.

Some items should already be listed in the text box. For example, either Client for NetWare or Client for Microsoft will be listed, depending on what type of file server you initially connected to. Also listed are your network interface card (adapter) and possibly the IPX/SPX (NetWare) or NetBeui (Microsoft) protocols. TCP/IP should be listed because you added it.

2. Click **OK** to close the Network dialog box.

3. Double-click **Network Neighborhood** to attempt to browse the network. You may or may not be able to browse at this point.

4. Right-click **Network Neighborhood** and click **Properties**.

5. Click on the **adapter** and then click **Properties**. Make sure the NIC is bound to the protocols. Click **OK**.

6. If you are on a NetWare network using IPX/SPX, click the **IPX/SPX** protocol and then click **Properties**. Click the **NetBios** tab and click the check box to enable NetBios over IPX/SPX. Click the **Bindings** tab and make sure any check boxes are checked. Click **OK**.

7. Click the **TCP/IP** protocol and then click **Properties**. Click the **IP Address** tab and type in the **IP address** and **subnet mask** per your instructor. If you are using DHCP, you choose the **Obtain an IP Address Automatically** option.

8. Click the **Bindings** tab and make sure the **Client** check box is checked.

9. If your instructor provided you with WINs and Gateway addresses, click those tabs and enter the numbers provided. Click **OK**.

10. Select your Primary Network Logon from the list box in the Network dialog box. It will probably be the Windows Logon, the Client for Microsoft Networks, or a Novell NetWare client.

11. Double-click the client in the Network Components list box. Complete any additional information your instructor gives you regarding the preferred server or domain.

12. Click **OK**, then **OK** again to exit the Network dialog box. If you are prompted for files, they are on drive C in the directory structure that you copied the Windows 95 installation files into.

13. Reboot when prompted.

14. Double-click **Network Neighborhood**. You should be able to see the names of other computers on the network. If you can't, begin troubleshooting with your instructor's help.

CHAPTER FIVE

NETWORK TOPOLOGY AND DESIGN

Labs included in this chapter

➤ Lab 5.1 Make and Test a Straight-through Patch Cable

➤ Lab 5.2 Make and Test a Crossover Patch Cable

➤ Lab 5.3 Identify Various Cable Types and Connectors

➤ Lab 5.4 Simulate a Network by Connecting a CSU/DSU, Router, Bridge, Three Hubs, and Nine Computers

➤ Lab 5.5 Subnet a Given IP Address and Assign Addresses to Computers and Interfaces in the Simulated Network

LAB 5.1 MAKE AND TEST A STRAIGHT-THROUGH PATCH CABLE

Objective

The objective of this lab is to teach you to make a typical UTP patch cable. Although you can readily purchase patch cables, making and testing one will give you insight to how UTP cable is made and how it operates. In this lab you will make a straight-through cable per the EIA/TIA 568B specifications shown in Figure 5-1. You will then test the cable using a simple continuity tester. After completing this lab you will be able to:

➤ Make a working patch cable per EIA/TIA 568B specifications.

➤ Test the cable for continuity.

➤ Troubleshoot problems such as no continuity or crossed pairs.

Materials Required

This lab requires:

➤ A box or spool of Cat 5 UTP cable

➤ One UTP cable crimper and one pair of wire cutters for every four students

➤ Box of RJ-45 connectors

➤ One UTP continuity tester for every four students

ACTIVITY

Make and Test a Straight-through Patch Cable

1. Score (do not penetrate) the jacket of the cable with the wire cutters at about 1.5" down. You will remove the outer jacket only, not the insulation on the individual wires.

2. Bend the cable gently at the score mark, and try to snap off the jacket.

3. Untwist all the wires down to the jacket.

4. Moving from left to right, put the wires in order. Use the EIA/TIA 568B standard colors shown in Figure 5-1.

EIA/TIA 568B Ethernet-data	White/ orange	Orange	White/ green	Blue	White/ blue	Green	White/ brown	Brown
EIA/TIA 568A voice & data	White/ green	Green	White/ orange	Blue	White/ blue	Orange	White/ brown	Brown

Figure 5-1   EIA/TIA Patch Cable Specifications

5. Use your thumb and third finger to flatten the wires.

6. Hold the wires flat and tightly together with the thumb and third finger of one hand, close to the base.

7. Use the wire cutters to snip the wires to about 0.5" above the base of the jacket.

8. Keep your grip on the wires while you slide the RJ-45 connector onto the ends of the wires. Make sure you still have the wires in the correct order. The clip of the connector should be down.

9. Slide the wires all the way in, and make sure the edge of the jacket slides just up under the edge of the connector about 0.25".

10. Slip the connector into the crimper tool. The clip of the connector should be down.

11. Keep your hands free of the blade as you squeeze the handles of the tool together until they release again.

12. Repeat Steps 1 through 11 for the other end of the wire. Use the same EIA/TIA 568B standard for this opposite end.

13. Now test your cable by inserting both ends of the cable into the tester. As you continually press the tester button, the indicator lights should light up to tell you that you have a good connection for each of the eight connections.

The lights should match if you made a successful, straight-through EIA/TIA cable; that is, light one on the left side should match up with light one on the right side. If light one matches up with light two, for example, you have crossed pairs.

14. If your cables fail the test, visually inspect the connector and make sure the color-coding is correct.

15. If the color-coding is correct, try re-crimping the connectors.

16. If the color-coding is incorrect, or re-crimping doesn't work, you'll have to cut the wire and start over. You cannot reuse the connector after it has been crimped.

Lab 5.2 Make and Test a Crossover Patch Cable

Objective

The objective of this lab is to teach you to make a crossover UTP patch cable. A crossover cable is required when connecting a hub to a hub. A crossover cable is also known as a *rollover cable* or *cross-connect cable*. Although you can readily purchase crossover cables, making and testing one will give you insight about how UTP cable is made and how a crossover cable differs from a straight-through cable. In this lab you will make a crossover cable per the EIA/TIA 568A and B specifications shown in Figure 5-1, Lab 5.1. You will then test the cable using a simple continuity tester. After completing this lab you will be able to:

➤ Make a working crossover cable per EIA/TIA 568A and B specifications.

➤ Test the cable for continuity.

➤ Troubleshoot problems such as no continuity or crossed pairs.

Materials Required

This lab requires:

➤ A box or spool of Cat 5 UTP cable

➤ One UTP cable crimper and one pair of wire cutters for every four students

➤ Box of RJ-45 connectors

➤ One UTP continuity tester for every four students

Activity

Make and Test a Crossover Patch Cable

1. Score (do not penetrate) the jacket of the cable with the wire cutters at about 1.5" down. You will remove the outer jacket only, not the insulation on the individual wires.

2. Bend the cable gently at the score mark, and try to snap off the jacket.

3. Untwist all the wires down to the jacket.

4. Moving from left to right, put the wires in order. Use the EIA/TIA 568B standard colors shown in Figure 5-1, Lab 5.1.

5. Use your thumb and third finger to flatten the wires.

6. Hold the wires flat and tightly together with the thumb and third finger of one hand, close to the base.

7. Use the wire cutters to snip the wires to about 0.5" above the base of the jacket.

8. Keep your grip on the wires while you slide the RJ-45 connector onto the ends of the wires. Make sure you still have the wires in the correct order. The clip of the connector should be down.

9. Slide the wires all the way in, and make sure the edge of the jacket slides just up under the edge of the connector about 0.25".

10. Slip the connector into the crimper tool. The clip of the connector should be down.

11. Keep your hands free of the blade as you squeeze the handles of the tool together until they release again.

12. Repeat Steps 1 through 11 for the other end of the wire, but this time use the color configuration that corresponds to the EIA/TIA 568A standard in Figure 5–1, Lab 5.1. This will make the cable a crossover cable.

13. Now test your cable by inserting both ends of the cable into the tester. As you continually press the tester button, the indicator lights should light up to tell you that you have a good connection for each of the eight connections.

If you made a successful crossover cable, the lights for one and three should match up and the lights for two and six should match, as shown in Figure 5-2.

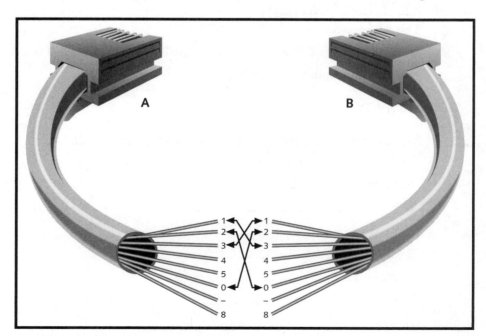

Figure 5-2   Successful crossover cable

14. If your cables fail the test, visually inspect the connector and make sure the color-coding is correct.

15. If the color-coding is correct, try re-crimping the connectors.

16. If the color-coding is not correct, or re-crimping doesn't work, you'll have to cut the wire and start over. You cannot reuse the connector after it has been crimped.

LAB 5.3 IDENTIFY VARIOUS CABLE TYPES AND CONNECTORS

Objective

The objective of this lab is to help you become familiar with various cable types and connectors that might be part of a LAN. In this lab your instructor will label examples of LAN cable and connectors. You will match the labeled LAN hardware with the descriptions below. After completing this lab you will be able to:

➤ Identify various cable types and connectors that are part of typical LAN installations.

Materials Required

This lab requires:

➤ Examples of cable and connectors listed below and labeled from A – J.

➤ This lab manual and a pencil

ACTIVITY

Match the labeled connectors and cable with the descriptions below.

A. thinnet _____

B. thicknet _____

C. cat 5 _____

D. cat 3 _____

E. multimode fiber _____

F. single-mode fiber _____

G. STP _____

H. T- connector _____

I. RJ-45 connector _____

J. RG-58 terminator _____

LAB 5.4 SIMULATE A NETWORK BY CONNECTING A CSU/DSU, ROUTER, BRIDGE, THREE HUBS, AND NINE COMPUTERS

Objective

The objective of this lab is to provide you with the opportunity to connect a network using various WAN and LAN hardware. Although this is just a simulation, it will give you insight into the hardware connections required in a LAN/WAN relationship. Figure 5-3 shows the exact configuration. In this lab you will connect a CSU/DSU to a router with a standard serial cable. The router will then be connected to two hubs via Ethernet ports. On one side of the router there will be two hubs separated by a bridge. There is an additional hub on the other side of the router. You may simulate the nine workstations on the hubs using old NIC cards. After completing this lab you will be able to:

➤ Identify various WAN and LAN devices.

➤ Connect the WAN and LAN devices as shown in Figure 5-3.

Materials Required

This lab requires:

➤ One CSU/DSU (may substitute a router if necessary)

➤ One Cisco router with two Ethernet ports and at least one serial port

➤ Three hubs

➤ One bridge (may substitute a switch if necessary)

➤ Nine NIC cards to simulate nine host computers

➤ Up to nine transceivers (if necessary to accommodate the UTP connections to old NICs with no RJ-45 transceivers)

➤ Nine UTP patch cables

➤ One serial cable

➤ UTP and/or thinnet for connections between the router, hubs, and bridge

➤ Any necessary BNC connectors and terminators if using thinnet

ACTIVITY

Simulate a Network by Connecting a CSU/DSU, Router, Bridge, Three Hubs, and Nine Computers

1. Lay out the devices on a table as shown in Figure 5-3.

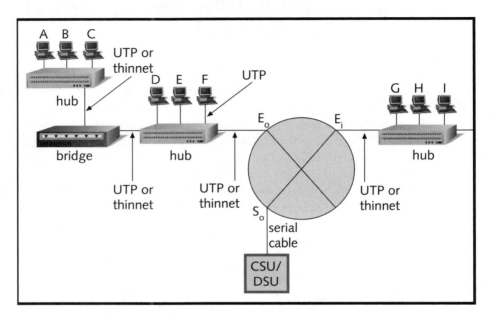

Figure 5-3 Network number 204.106.37.0

2. Connect the CSU/DSU to a serial interface on the router using the serial cable.

3. Connect an Ethernet port on the router to a hub using thinnet or UTP cable.

4. Connect the other Ethernet port on the router to another hub using thinnet or UTP cable.

5. Connect the hub on the left to the bridge using thinnet or UTP cable. There may be a switch on the bridge that needs to be configured, depending on the type of cable you have connected to it. Make sure the switch is in the correct position.

6. Connect the bridge to the next hub using thinnet or UTP cable.

7. Connect three patch cables to a hub using UTP patch cables. Make sure none of the patch cables are connected to the uplink port of the hub. The uplink port is used for hub-to-hub connections when using a straight-through patch cable instead of a crossover cable. You cannot use this port for workstations. The uplink port is usually marked. Sometimes there is a switch that can be positioned to configure a regular port as an uplink port.

8. Now connect the other end of the patch cables used in Step 7 to the NICs to simulate connecting workstations. If you are using old NICs, they may not have an RJ-45 transceiver. In this case, you will need to use a BNC or AUI to RJ-45 transceiver between the patch cable and the NIC.

9. Repeat Steps 7 and 8 for the other hubs and NICs to complete your simulated network.

LAB 5.5 SUBNET A GIVEN IP ADDRESS AND ASSIGN ADDRESSES TO COMPUTERS AND INTERFACES IN THE SIMULATED NETWORK

Objective

The objective of this lab is to provide you with another opportunity to practice IP subnetting. In this lab you will use the subnetting formulas you learned in Chapter 3 to subnet the given network number 204.106.37.0. You will provide IP addresses for the serial and Ethernet interfaces and the workstations you connected in Lab 5.4. You should borrow the minimum number of bits required when subnetting. After completing this lab you will be able to:

➤ Create an efficient IP addressing scheme for all the interfaces on the simulated network in Lab 5.4.

Materials Required

This lab requires:

➤ The simulated network configured in Lab 5-4

➤ This lab manual

➤ Sticky labels and a pencil

ACTIVITY

1. How many bits will you borrow? _____

2. What is the subnet mask? _____

3. What are the addresses for the Ethernet and serial interfaces? _____

   _____

   _____

4. What are the addresses for the hosts? _____

   _____

   _____

5. What is the broadcast address for the Ethernet subnets? _____

   _____

   _____

6. Use sticky labels to identify the locations on the simulated network interfaces and their corresponding IP addresses.

MEDIA INSTALLATION

Labs included in this chapter

➤ Lab 6.1 Punch Down and Test UTP Cable

➤ Lab 6.2 Determine the Number and Locations of Wiring Closets Required for an Ethernet LAN with an Extended Star Topology

➤ Lab 6.3 Determine MCC, ICC, and HCC Locations for a Campus LAN

➤ Lab 6.4 Use an Advanced Cable Tester to Troubleshoot Network Cable

LAB 6.1 PUNCH DOWN AND TEST UTP CABLE

Objective

The purpose of this lab is to familiarize you with a patch panel and to teach you to punch down and test cable. In this lab you will use the EIA/TIA 568B specification to make one end of a patch cable. You will connect the other end to the pin side of the patch panel using the proper technique. You will finish by testing your connection for continuity. After completing this lab you will be able to:

➤ Punch down UTP cable into a patch panel.

➤ Test the connection using a simple cable tester.

Materials Required

This lab requires:

➤ One patch panel for every four students, preferably mounted on a rack to hold it steady

➤ One Krone tool or other punchdown tool for every four students

➤ Spool of cat 5 UTP cable

➤ RJ-45 connectors

➤ One pair of wire cutters for every four students

ACTIVITY

Punch Down and Test UTP Cable

1. Make one end of an EIA/TIA 568B patch cable following the specifications in Figure 6-1.

EIA/TIA 568B Ethernet-data	White/ orange	Orange	White/ green	Blue	White/ blue	Green	White/ brown	Brown
EIA/TIA 568A voice & data	White/ green	Green	White/ orange	Blue	White/ blue	Orange	White/ brown	Brown

Figure 6-1   EIA/TIA patch cable specifications

2. At the end with no connector, score (do not penetrate) the jacket of the cable with the wire cutters at about 1.5" down. You will remove the outer jacket only, not the insulation on the individual wires.

3. Bend the cable gently at the score mark, and try to snap off the jacket.

4. Untwist the wires as little as possible.

5. Moving from left to right, line up wire colors with the punch-down block pin colors. The striped wires go to the left of the pin; the solid color wires go to the right of the pin.

6. Push the wires between the pins, being careful to keep the correct color order. Only 0.25" of wire should be exposed between the cable jacket and the pins. Let the rest of the wire stick out above the pins.

7. Keep the cable centered about the pins. If the cable becomes skewed to the right or left, network performance will be affected.

8. Position the punch-down tool over the first wire. The cut side of the tool should face up.

9. Position the tool perpendicular to the block. Push into the wire with the tool.

10. The excess wire above the block should snap off. If it doesn't, you can twist it off with your fingers.

11. Continue punching down the rest of the wires.

12. When you finish, you should have a UTP cable attached at one end to the punch-down block. An RJ-45 connector should be at the other end.

13. To test the continuity of the connection, connect a regular EIA/TIA 568B patch cable to the port on the other side of the punch-down block that corresponds to the pin you have wired.

14. Plug the end of the patch cable that is connected to the port into a cable tester.

15. Plug the patch cable that is connected to the pin side of the block into the cable tester.

16. Each time you press the test button, the indicator lights should light to tell you that you have a good connection for that particular pair of wires.

17. If your cables fail the test, start troubleshooting with the help of your instructor.

LAB 6.2 DETERMINE THE NUMBER AND LOCATIONS OF WIRING CLOSETS REQUIRED FOR AN ETHERNET LAN WITH AN EXTENDED STAR TOPOLOGY

Objective

The objective of this lab is to help you determine the best location for a wiring closet, given the single-story LAN shown in Figure 6-2. The letters A through E in the figure represent possible wiring closet locations. In this lab you will determine the best locations for the MDF and the IDF based on EIA/TIA specifications for UTP cable. After completing this lab you will:

➤ Understand the factors involved in determining the best locations for wiring closets

➤ Understand the relationship between the POP and the MDF

➤ Understand the relationship between the MDF and the IDF

Materials Required

This lab requires:

➤ A ruler for every four students

➤ A compass for drawing circles for every four students

➤ This lab manual and a pencil

ACTIVITY

Determine the Number and Locations of Wiring Closets Required for an Ethernet LAN with an Extended Star Topology

1. Make sure the compass is fitted with a sharpened pencil.

2. You need to draw circles with a radius of 50 meters from each of the proposed wiring closet locations indicated by the letters A through E in Figure 6-2. Because the scale is 50 meters per 2.25", extend your compass to 2.25".

3. Why are you drawing circles with a 50-meter radius instead of the 100-meter limitation for UTP? _____

   _____

   _____

   _____

4. Push the sharp point of the compass into the center of closet A. Use the compass to draw a circle around this point.

5. Label a few points on the circle with As, so you do not confuse circle A with circles B, C, D, and E, which you will draw next.

6. Repeat Steps 4 and 5 for positions B through E.

7. How many wiring closets do you need to provide a big enough catchment area? _____

8. Where will you put the MDF? Why? _____

   _____

   _____

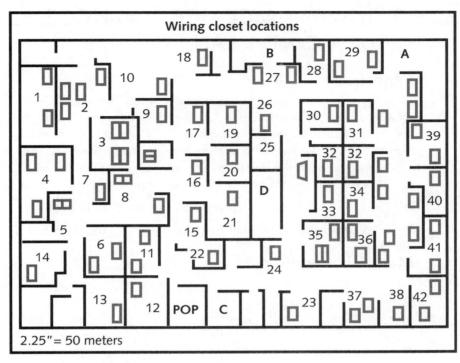

Figure 6-2 Wiring closet locations

9. Where will you put the IDF? Why? _____

   _____

   _____

10. If only a few devices are moved, will any wiring closet location provide a
    large enough catchment area so that only one closet will be required? If
    so, which closet is it? Which rooms are not covered? _____

    _____

    _____

    _____

11. How does your wiring closet decision change if you learn that closet E has
    fluorescent lighting and that steam pipes run through closet D? _____

    _____

    _____

    _____

    _____

12. What is the advantage or disadvantage to using location C for the MDF?

    _____

    _____

    _____

LAB 6.3 DETERMINE MCC, ICC, AND HCC LOCATIONS FOR A CAMPUS LAN

Objective

The objective of this lab is to help you determine the best MCC, ICC, and HCC locations for the campus LAN illustrated in Figure 6-3. In this lab you will label the best locations for the MCC, ICC, and HCCs, then draw solid lines to identify the backbone cabling between these closets. Assume multimode fiber between the buildings and between any ICCs and HCCs. Assume cat 5 UTP for the horizontal cabling. After completing this lab you will:

➤ Understand the relationship between the MCC and the POP.

➤ Understand the relationship between the MCC, the ICCs and the HCCs.

Materials Required

This lab requires:

➤ A ruler for every student

➤ A compass for every four students

➤ This lab manual and a pencil

ACTIVITY

Determine MCC, ICC, and HCC Locations for a Campus LAN

1. Label the best location for the MCC on your Figure 6.3. Why did you choose this location? _____
   _____
   _____

2. Label the ICCs in the buildings. In Figure 6-3, small circles identify the existing closet locations which can serve as these ICCs.

3. Use the compass to draw circles with a 50-meter radius around the ICCs. Determine if one closet will suffice for any of the buildings. Is it possible to use HCCs in any of the buildings instead of ICCs? _____
   If you can use some HCCs in place of ICCs, re-label those closets as HCCs.

4. Use solid lines to identify the backbone cabling between the MCC and the existing closets. Consider that running multiple cables in the same trench saves money.

5. What is the distance limitation on multimode fiber used as backbone cabling between the MCC and the ICCs? _____

_____

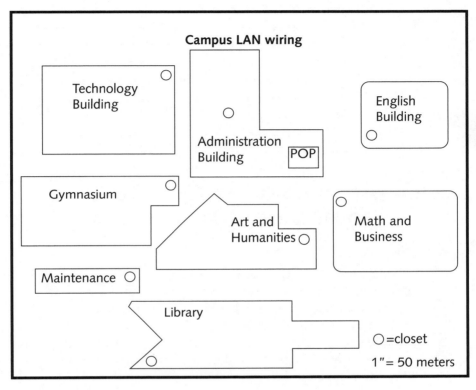

Figure 6-3 Campus LAN wiring

6. Do multimode fiber distance limitations present a problem with this campus LAN? Why or why not? _____

_____

7. What is the distance limitation on multimode fiber used as backbone cabling between ICCs and HCCs? _____

_____

8. Use the compass again to locate additional closet locations for HCCs in each building as necessary. Mark these locations with an X. Will any buildings need more than one HCC? If yes, which buildings? _____

_____

_____

9. Use dashed lines to identify the backbone cabling between the ICCs and the HCCs.

10. Is it possible to run cat 5 UTP cable between any of the buildings? Why or why not? _____

_____

_____

_____

11. Is it possible to run category 5 UTP cable between any of the ICCs and the HCCs? If yes, in which buildings? _____

_____

_____

_____

LAB 6.4 USE AN ADVANCED CABLE TESTER TO TROUBLESHOOT NETWORK CABLE

Objective

The objective of this lab is to provide you with an opportunity to use an advanced cable tester to perform various tests. Cable testers vary in their abilities to test and troubleshoot cable. You may or may not be able to perform all tests with your particular advanced cable tester. Activities for this lab include general network diagnostics; monitoring activity on your LAN; testing cabling, connections, and hub ports; producing a wire map, and testing for crosstalk. After completing this lab you will:

➤ Understand the general abilities of an advanced network cable tester

Materials Required

This lab requires:

➤ An advanced cable tester

ACTIVITY

Diagnosing the Network

1. Connect the cable tester to an RJ-45 telecommunications connector with a patch cable.

2. Turn on the cable tester.

3. Press the Diagnose button if you have one. If you have no Diagnose button, ask the instructor to show you how to use your tester to answer common network questions such as, "Are the servers OK?" or "Why is the network slow?" Full server diagnosis may not be possible without first loading particular diagnostic software on the servers.

Looking at Network Traffic

1. Connect the cable tester to an RJ-45 telecommunications connector with a patch cable.

2. Ask your instructor to show you how to determine current segment utilization and error rate and how to monitor this data over time. On the Compass Ethernet cable tester, press a button marked "10101010" to get his information.

3. The monitor should begin collecting new data. After you stop data collection, many testers let you print the information.

4. On the Compass Ethernet cable tester, you can get segment utilization details at this point. It is important to know the "top talkers," top protocols, top error sources, and top broadcasters. Ask your instructor to demonstrate how to get information that is as detailed as possible.

Wire Maps

1. Attach the two ends of an RJ-5 patch cable to the cable tester's two RJ-45 connectors.

2. Ask your instructor to demonstrate how to display a wire map of the cable. On the Compass Ethernet cable tester, a button with a picture of a spool of cable on it serves this purpose. If there are any faults in the cable, the wire map shows them graphically.

Cable Testing

1. Most cable testers perform additional tests on the cable. Connect the cable tester to an RJ-45 telecommunications connector with a patch cable.

2. The Compass Ethernet cable tester has a button with a picture of a spool of cable on it. Press this button to put the attached cable under test.

3. The Compass Ethernet cable tester also usually has a menu button that gives you additional cable testing options; typically a crosstalk test, a noise test, and a trace cable option. Ask your instructor to demonstrate the additional tests you can perform on the cable using your particular advanced cable tester.

Server Summary

1. With the UTP patch cable still connecting the advanced cable tester to the telecommunications outlet, you can usually get server information on your network. The Compass Ethernet cable tester has a button with a picture of computers on it. Press this button to display data on the LAN servers. Don't be surprised if only Novell servers or only NT servers show on a Novell/NT LAN. Many cable testers are specific to the network operating system being used.

2. Ask your instructor to demonstrate the server information you can display with your particular advanced cable tester. The Compass Ethernet cable tester displays server name, frame type, number of routers between the tester and the server (measured in hops), and network speed.

3. More detailed server statistics are usually available. Typically, you can highlight a specific server and press a detail button for statistics such as processor utilization, connections in use, and server memory. The Compass Ethernet cable tester allows you to log on to a particular server with a legitimate user name and password.

Detect MAC Address

1. The Compass Ethernet cable tester lets you determine the MAC address on a workstation. Connect the tester to the workstation NIC using either thinnet (BNC connector) or UTP (RJ-45 connector).

2. Ask your instructor to demonstrate how to detect a MAC address using your particular advanced cable tester.

3. Reboot the workstation, or otherwise cause it to transmit a packet on the network. The cable tester should display the MAC address of the attached workstation.

7

ELECTRICITY AND ELECTRONICS

Labs included in this chapter

➤ Lab 7.1 Determine MCC, ICC, and HCC Locations for a Multistory LAN with Different Grounds

➤ Lab 7.2 Use a Voltmeter to Test Voltage at a Wall Outlet

Lab 7.1 Determine MCC, ICC, and HCC Locations for a Multistory LAN with Different Grounds

Objective

The objective of this lab is to help you determine the relationship between the MCC, ICCs, and HCCs for the multistory LAN shown in Figure 7-1. In this lab you will determine the best locations for the MCC, ICCs, and HCCs for companies A and B, which occupy several floors of the building. Company A occupies floors 1 through 49 of the building. Company B occupies the top 20 floors. Assume that no floor's area is greater than 1000 square meters. You will also determine what kind of cable will run between various closets. To reduce costs, you should use UTP whenever you can. After completing this lab you will:

➤ Understand the factors involved in determining the best locations for wiring closets in a multistory building.

➤ Understand the relationship between the POP and the MCC.

➤ Understand the relationship between the MCC, ICCs, and HCCs.

➤ Understand the difference between the MCC, ICC, HCC, MDF, and IDF.

Materials Required

This lab requires:

➤ This lab manual and a pencil

Activity

Determine MCC, ICC, and HCC Locations for a Multistory LAN with Different Grounds

Company B

1. Refer to Figure 7-1 to determine approximately on which floor the main wiring closet will be for Company B. _____

2. Label the wiring closet on Figure 7-1.

3. Draw a solid line between the POP and the main wiring closet for Company B.

4. What cable type will run between the POP and the main closet? Why?

_____

_____

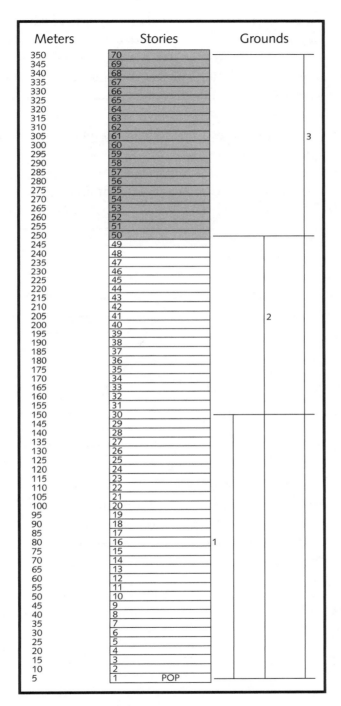

Figure 7-1   Multistory LAN

5. Are any ICCs necessary for the Company B LAN? Why or why not?

_____

_____

6. In this situation, will you use MCC and HCC terminology or MDF and IDF terminology? Why? _____

_____

7. What cable type will you use between the closets on the Company B LAN? Why? _____

_____

8. Did the grounding situation factor into any of your decisions for Company B? Why or why not? _____

_____

_____

Company A

9. Figure 7-1 shows the POP is on the first floor. Approximately where will the MCC be? Why? _____

_____

_____

10. Write MCC on the appropriate floor on Figure 7-1.

11. Draw a solid line between the MCC and POP. What type of cable will this be? Why? _____

_____

_____

12. Where will the HCCs be for Company A? _____

_____

13. On which floors are ICCs required? Can any wiring runs between the MCC and the ICCs be UTP? Why or why not? _____

_____

_____

_____

14. Label the ICCs on Figure 7-1. Draw solid lines between the MCC and the ICCs. Mark each run with either an "F" for fiber or "U" for UTP.

15. Which HCCs can be serviced with UTP from the MCC? _____

_____

_____

_____

16. How did the different grounds affect your decisions? _____

_____

_____

_____

LAB 7.2 USE A VOLTMETER TO TEST VOLTAGE AT A WALL OUTLET

Objective

The objective of this lab is to help you become familiar with the relationship between the three wires typically run to your home to provide alternating current to your household devices. In this lab you will use a standard voltmeter such as the one shown in Figure 7-2 to test for common mode and normal mode problems at a wall outlet. After completing this lab you will be able to:

➤ Use a voltmeter.

➤ Test for common mode problems at an outlet.

➤ Test for normal mode problems at an outlet.

Materials Required

This lab requires:

➤ Analog or digital voltmeter for every four students

➤ This lab manual and a pencil

ACTIVITY

Common Mode

1. To check the voltage between the neutral wire and the safety ground, begin by turning on the voltmeter. Then set the voltmeter to ACV (alternating current volts).

2. Make sure that the number you select is above 120. Most voltmeters have a setting of 200 or 250, which is sufficient.

3. A line on an analog voltmeter corresponds to AC readings. Find the line and notice the scale.

4. Insert one lead from the voltmeter into the upper-left opening in the socket (neutral) and the other into the bottom opening in the socket (safety ground), as shown in Figure 7-2.

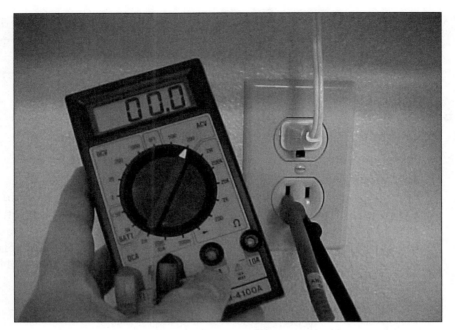

Figure 7-2 Voltage reading between neutral wire and safety ground

5. Check your voltmeter. It should show a reading of no more than 0.5 volts.

6. Why should the voltmeter show less than 0.5 volts when measuring the potential between the neutral wire and the safety ground? _____

_____

_____

_____

7. Why are common mode problems considered serious, especially for network administrators? _____

_____

_____

_____

_____

Normal Mode

1. To check the voltage between the hot lead wire and the neutral wire, begin by setting the meter to ACV (alternating current volts).

2. Insert one lead from the voltmeter into the upper-left opening in the socket (neutral) and the other into the upper-right opening in the socket (hot lead), as shown in Figure 7-3. As you do this, make sure to keep your fingers away from the metal ends of the voltmeter; otherwise, you may get a shock.

Figure 7-3 Voltage reading between neutral wire and hot lead wire

3. Check your voltmeter. It should show a reading of approximately 110 volts for a standard household or office outlet.

4. Why should the voltmeter show approximately 110 volts when measuring the potential between the hot lead wire and the neutral wire? _____

_____

_____

_____

5. Why are normal mode problems less serious than common mode problems? _____

_____

_____

_____

6. List some typical normal mode problems. _____

_____

_____

7. How can you prevent the problems you listed above? _____

_____

_____

_____

_____

WAN CONCEPTS

Labs included in this chapter

➤ Lab 9.1 Identify Connection Methods Used with WAN Data Link Protocols

➤ Lab 9.2 Understand Packet-Switching Terminology

➤ Lab 9.3 Associate WAN Technologies with the Appropriate Layer of the OSI Reference Model

LAB 9.1 IDENTIFY CONNECTION METHODS USED WITH WAN DATA LINK PROTOCOLS

Objective

The objective of this lab is to clarify the relationship between WAN data link protocols and the connection methods with which they are typically used. In this lab you will define the protocol acronyms and indicate whether a particular WAN data-link protocol is associated with point-to-point, multipoint, or switched connection methods. After completing this lab you will:

➤ Understand the three connection methods used in WAN transmission.

➤ Understand the various data-link protocols associated with the WAN connection methods.

Materials Required

This lab requires:

➤ This lab manual and a pencil

ACTIVITY

Below each of the WAN data-link protocols listed, define the acronym. Then, choose the WAN connection method that applies to each protocol: point-to-point, multipoint, or switched. One protocol may be associated with more than one connection method.

   1. ISDN

      _____

      _____

   2. SDLC

      _____

      _____

   3. PPP

      _____

      _____

   4. X.25

      _____

      _____

   5. ATM

      _____

      _____

6. HDLC

_____

_____

7. Frame Relay

_____

_____

Lab 9.2 Understand Packet-Switching Terminology

Objective

The objective of this lab is to help you learn the terminology and definitions associated with packet-switching technologies. In this lab you will match the correct packet-switching term with a definition. After completing this lab you will:

➤ Understand characteristics of packet-switching technologies.

➤ Relate packet-switching terms to the technology with which they are associated.

Materials Required

This lab requires:

➤ This lab manual and a pencil

Activity

Match each definition in the numbered list with a term from the list below:

X.25	BECN
LAPB	FECN
Inverse ARP	D–channel
DLCI	B–channel
Frame Relay	X.21
SVC	LAPD
PVC	Cell
CIR	CSU/DSU
LMI	Synchronous
ISDN	Asynchronous
BRI	Terminal adapter
ATM	Packet-switched

9

1. Type of network in which relatively small units of data are routed through a network based on the destination address. This type of communication is connectionless rather than dedicated. _____

2. LAN and WAN protocol that handles digital data transmission up to 622 Mbps. Requires dedicated hardware. _____

3. ITU standard for digital transmission over ordinary telephone wires, in addition to other media. Transmission speeds are up to 128 Kbps for home use. _____

4. Hardware that converts digital data frames from a LAN into frames appropriate for a WAN and vice versa. _____

5. Cost-efficient data transmission between LANs and WANs. Uses a variable-size packet and leaves any necessary error correction to the upper-layer protocols. _____

6. Service consisting of two 64 Kbps B-channels and one 16 Kbps D-channel. _____

7. Keepalive mechanism that periodically sends the router status information regarding a transmission. _____

8. Allows frame relay station to discover the protocol address of a node associated with the virtual circuit. _____

9. Carries control and signaling information for ISDN. _____

10. Underlying data-link layer protocol for X.25. _____

11. Used to identify the PVC or SVC on a frame relay network.

   _____

12. Bandwidth associated with a logical connection in a frame relay network.

   _____

13. Term used for the fixed-length packet associated with ATM transmission.

   _____

14. Should result in router transmitting less traffic. _____

15. Relies on start and stop bits to define end points of a transmission.

   _____

16. Physical layer standard that defines the interface between the DTE and the DCE. _____

17. Warns the next router that congestion has been experienced.

   _____

18. Underlying protocol for transmission over ISDN lines.

   _____

19. A WAN connection that the network administrator sets up, which performs as if it were a dedicated line. _____

20. Used to transfer data over ISDN lines. _____

21. Temporary circuit created when the network calls the WAN. _____
_____

22. Interface between a computer and an ISDN line. Replaces a modem.
_____

23. Data-link protocol originally developed to work over existing analog phone lines. Uses extensive error checking. _____

24. Communications that rely on a clock. _____

Lab 9.3 Associate WAN Technologies with the Appropriate Layer of the OSI Reference Model

9

Objective

The objective of this lab is to learn where WAN technologies fit into the OSI reference model. In this lab you will indicate at which OSI layer or layers the listed WAN technology resides. After completing this lab you will:

➤ Understand where various WAN technologies fit into the OSI reference model.

Materials Required

This lab requires:

➤ This lab manual and a pencil

Activity

Next to each WAN technology listed, write at which layer or layers of the OSI reference model the technology resides.

RS-232 _____

X.25 _____

LAPD _____

HSSI _____

Frame Relay _____

SDLC _____

X.21 _____

V.35 _____

PPP _____

HDLC _____

ATM _____

EIA–530 _____

ROUTER BASICS

Labs included in this chapter

➤ Lab 10.1 Connect the Cisco Networking Academies Semester 2 Internetwork Lab

➤ Lab 10.2 Configure Hyperterminal to Access a Cisco Router

➤ Lab 10.3 Use the System Configuration Dialog to Configure a Cisco Router

➤ Lab 10.4 Configure Console and Aux Passwords

➤ Lab 10.5 Use HELP, the Command History, Enhanced Editing Features, and the Show Command

LAB 10.1 CONNECT THE CISCO NETWORKING ACADEMIES SEMESTER 2 INTERNETWORK LAB

Objective

The objective of this lab is to give you experience in making the hardware connections necessary to configure the Cisco router lab. This includes connecting computers, hubs, and routers to each other. In this lab you will connect five Cisco routers, five hubs, and five computers in preparation for router configuration. After completing this lab you will be able to:

➤ Identify routers, hubs, transceivers, DCE/DTE cables, rollover cables, DB25 connectors, and the COM2 port on the computers.

➤ Correctly connect the hardware via the proper cables.

Materials Required

This lab requires the Cisco Networking Academies hardware package which includes:

➤ Four, 2501 series routers with power cables

➤ One, 2514 series router with power cable

➤ Five hubs with power cables

➤ Three V.35 DTE cables (male)

➤ Three V.35 DCE cables (female)

➤ Six UTP patch cables

➤ Six Ethernet 10BaseT UTP to AUI transceivers

➤ Five RJ-45 to RJ-45 rollover cables

➤ Five RJ-45 to DB-25 or DB-9 connectors

➤ Power strips

In addition, you need:

➤ Five Windows 95/98 computers with the COM2 port available. Computers should be set up in a line and labeled A through E, as shown in Figure 10-1.

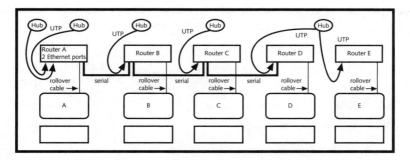

Figure 10-1 Standard network configuration

➤ Routers labeled A through E. Router A should be the series 2514 router.

➤ A second long table behind the computers to lay out the routers and associated hardware

ACTIVITY

1. Lay the five routers on the long table behind the computers with the routers' port sides facing the back of the computers. The 2514 router should be behind computer A. The router labeled B should be behind computer B and so forth.

2. Place a hub behind each router.

3. Refer to Figure 10-2 for additional connection information.

10

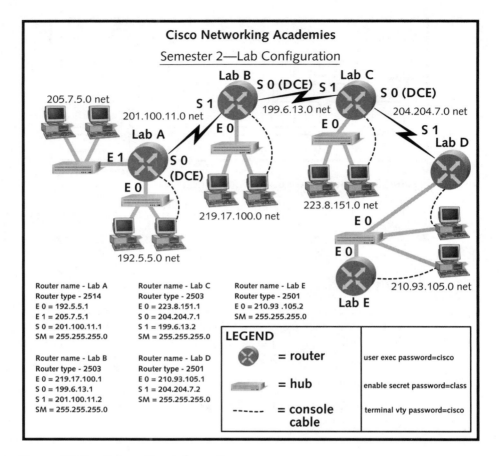

Figure 10-2 Connection information

4. Connect router A to the hub behind it using a UTP patch cable. You need a transceiver between the AUI-0 port on the router and the RJ-45 connector. At the hub, make sure the UTP is not plugged into an uplink port. Ask your instructor for help if you cannot determine which port is the uplink port.

5. Connect router A to a second hub via its AUI-1 port in the same manner outlined in Step 4.

6. Connect router B to a third hub as outlined in Step 4.

7. Connect router C to a fourth hub as outlined in Step 4.

8. Connect routers D and E to the fifth hub as outlined in Step 4 and shown in Figure 10-2.

9. Connect the console port of router A to the COM2 port of computer A using the router rollover cable. At the COM2 port, you need a DB-25 or DB-9 connector between the RJ-45 rollover cable and the COM2 port.

10. Repeat Step 9 for routers B through E.

11. The DTE and DCE cables should be marked as such. Connect each DTE cable to a DCE cable. You should now have three cables, each with a DTE end and a DCE end.

12. The 60-pin ends of the DTE and DCE serial cables should be connected to the serial ports on the routers. Connect router A to router B using Figure 10-2 as a reference. Notice that the DCE end goes in router A's S0 port, and the DTE end goes in router B's S1 port.

13. Repeat Step 12 to connect router B to router C, and then to connect router C to router D.

14. Connect all devices to the power strips using the correct power cables.

15. Ask your instructor to check your lab setup.

LAB 10.2 CONFIGURE HYPERTERMINAL TO ACCESS A CISCO ROUTER

10

Objective

The objective of this lab is to give you experience configuring the Windows 95/98 Hyperterminal program, which is frequently used to configure routers. In this lab you will configure Hyperterminal on a computer connected to a router via the console port. You performed this hardware setup in Lab 10-1. After completing Lab 10.2 you will be able to:

➤ Configure Hyperterminal on a Windows 95/98 computer for use in configuring Cisco routers.

Materials Required

This lab requires:

➤ The Cisco Networking Academies Semester 2 Internetworking Lab setup in Lab 10-1 and shown in Figure 10-2, or a Windows 95/98 computer connected to a Cisco router via the console port on the router

ACTIVITY

1. Make sure the router connected to the computer is turned off.

2. Turn on the Windows 95/98 computer.

3. Click **Start,** then click **Programs, Accessories,** and **Hyperterminal**. On a Windows 98 computer, Hyperterminal is in the Communications folder.

4. Double-click the **Hypertrm** program to open the New Connection window.

5. The Hyperterminal Wizard may launch at this point and prompt you for input. The following steps list the required input. You may need to click **File** and then click **New Connection** if the New Connection window doesn't open.

6. Enter the name **Cisco** for the connection. Click **OK** to continue.

7. You must now configure how you will connect to the router via the Connect To dialog box. In the **Connect using** selection box, choose the Com Port to which the RJ-45 to DB-9 or DB-25 connector is attached. Click **OK** to continue.

8. Configure these settings for the COM port: Bits per second: **9600**; Data bits: **8**; Stop bits: **1**; Parity: **None**; Flow control: **Xon/Xoff**. Click **OK** to complete the configuration.

9. Click **File,** then click **Save** to save the connection.

10. Close Hyperterminal, then double-click the connection to reopen it.

11. Turn on the connected router.

12. Watch for the router start-up information. You may need to press **Enter** key on the computer keyboard to initiate this process.

13. When you know Hyperterminal is correctly configured, you may turn off the router and exit Windows 95/98.

LAB 10.3 USE THE SYSTEM CONFIGURATION DIALOG TO CONFIGURE A CISCO ROUTER

Objective

The objective of this lab is to give you experience with the initial configuration of a Cisco router using the System Configuration Dialog. Remember that setting up the router using this method makes the router operational; however, it is not completely configured. You can complete the Cisco Networking Academies configuration in the Chapter 11 labs. In this lab you will use the System Configuration Dialog to configure as much as you can of the Cisco

Networking Academies Semester 2 Lab. After completing this lab you will be able to:

➤ Use the System Configuration Dialog to configure the routers in the Cisco Networking Academies Semester 2 Lab.

Materials Required

This lab requires:

➤ The Cisco Networking Academies Semester 2 Lab setup per Figure 10-2 and Lab 10-1

➤ Hyperterminal configured to access the routers via the console port per Lab 10-2

ACTIVITY

1. The router's start-up configuration file should already be erased. Doing so makes the router enter set-up mode when it is turned on.

2. Turn the router off if it is on.

3. Boot the attached computer into Windows 95/98. To open the Hyperterminal connection you created in Lab 10-2, click **Start**, click **Programs**, click **Accessories**, then click **Hyperterminal**. Double-click the **Cisco** connection icon. Remember, on a Windows 98 computer, the Hyperterminal program is in the Communications folder instead of the Accessories folder.

4. Turn on the router attached to your PC. Press **Enter**. In a few minutes you should see router activity display.

5. You should see a message that the NVRAM is invalid, possibly due to write erase. That is because your instructor has erased the start-up configuration file or because the router never had a start-up configuration.

6. Next, you will be asked if you want to enter the initial configuration dialog. The default is yes, so just press **Enter**.

7. When asked if you would like to see the current interface summary, press **n** for no and press **Enter**.

8. To configure the router per Figure 10-2, follow the instructions in Table 10-1. Configure all interfaces that you are prompted to configure if, and only if, they are configured per Figure 10-2.

10

Table 10-1 Steps to configure the router

Question	Explanation
Enter host name [Router]:	The host name is the name of your router. Type the name of your router, and press **Enter**. If you are using the Cisco Networking Academies Semester 2 Lab setup, the router name is probably lab-a, lab-b, lab-c, lab-d, or lab-e.
Enter enable secret:	The enable secret password for the Cisco Networking Academies Semester 2 Lab setup is **class**. Type the password, then press **Enter**.
Enter enable password:	Type **cisco** and press **Enter**.
Enter virtual terminal password:	Type **cisco** and press **Enter**.
Configure SNMP Network Management? [yes]:	Type **n** for no and press **Enter**.
Configure Vines? [no]:	Press **Enter** to accept the default, [no].
Configure LAT? [no]:	Press **Enter** to accept the default, [no].
Configure AppleTalk? [no]:	Press **Enter** to accept the default, [no].
Configure DECnet? [no]:	Press **Enter** to accept the default, [no].
Configure IP? [yes]:	Press **Enter** to accept the default, [yes].
Configure IGRP? [yes]:	Type **n** for no and press **Enter**.
Configure RIP routing? [no]:	Type **y** for yes and press **Enter**. You are prompted to enter the network numbers to which your router is **directly** connected. Refer to Figure 10-2, type each network number, and press **Enter**. Do not type in interface numbers.
Configure CLNS? [no]:	Press **Enter** to accept the default, [no].
Configure bridging? [no]:	Press **Enter** to accept the default, [no].
Configure IPX? [no]:	Press **Enter** to accept the default, [no].
Configure XNS? [no]:	Press **Enter** to accept the default, [no].
Configure Apollo? [no]:	Press **Enter** to accept the default, [no].
Configuring interface Ethernet0: Is this interface in use? [yes]	Press **Enter** to accept the default, [yes].
Configure IP on this interface? [yes]:	Press **Enter** to accept the default, [yes].
IP address for this interface:	Enter the IP address you want to assign to the Ethernet0 interface. Do not type a subnet mask. Press **Enter**.

Continued

Table 10-1 (continued)

Question	Explanation
Number of bits in the subnet field [0]:	Enter the number of bits that you want to use beyond the normal subnet mask. The IOS automatically subnets your address, based on the default subnet for the address class. In this case you should use zero, because the default subnet mask is being used. Press **Enter**.
Configuring interface Serial0: Is this interface in use? [yes]:	If you are going to use the Serial0 interface on the router (see Figure 10-2) press **Enter** to accept the default, [yes]. If not, type n for no and press **Enter**.
Configure IP on this interface?	You can decide whether to enable IP on the serial interface. If you choose yes, you will have to configure the IP settings. Again, refer to Figure 10-2 to determine if your router uses this interface.
Configure IP unnumbered on this interface? [no]:	Press **Enter** to accept the default, [no].
IP address for this interface:	Enter the IP address for the serial interface per Figure 10-2 if you are using it. Press **Enter**.
Number of bits in subnet field [0]:	Press **Enter** to accept the default, [0].
Use this configuration? [yes/no]	Type **yes** and press **Enter** if you believe you configured the router correctly. The router reboots. If you made errors and don't want to save the configuration, type **no** and press **Enter**. Turn the router off and on, and start again.

10

LAB 10.4 CONFIGURE CONSOLE AND AUX PASSWORDS

Objective

The objective of this lab is to give you experience in adding the additional router access passwords that are not configured when using the System Configuration Dialog. These additional passwords are the console password, which restricts access to User Exec mode and therefore also Privileged Exec mode, and the aux password. The aux password restricts access to the router via a modem. In this lab you will configure the console and aux passwords for the Cisco Networking Academies Semester 2 Lab. You may use different passwords if your instructor provides them. After completing this lab you will be able to:

➤ Configure the console and aux passwords on a router.

Materials Required

This lab requires:

➤ The Cisco Networking Academies Semester 2 Lab setup per Figure 10-2 and Lab 10.1

➤ Hyperterminal configured to access the routers via the console port per Lab 10.2

➤ The Cisco Networking Academies Semester 2 Lab configured per Lab 10.3

ACTIVITY

1. Boot the computer into Windows 95/98, and begin the Hyperterminal session with the router.

2. Turn on the router if necessary. Press **Enter** to get the User Exec mode prompt, which should be the name of the router (for example, lab-e) and the greater than sign (>).

3. Type **ena** and press **Enter** to access Privileged Exec mode.

4. Type **class** and press **Enter** when prompted for the password. The prompt should change. For example, if the router name is lab-e, the prompt should change to lab-e#.

5. Type **conf t** and press **Enter** to enter global configuration mode. The prompt should change. For example, if the router name is lab-e, the prompt should change to lab-e(config)#.

6. Type **line console 0** and press **Enter**. This tells the router that you want to configure the console port. The prompt should change. For example, if the router name is lab-e, the prompt should change to lab-e(config-line)#.

7. Type **login** and press **Enter**.

8. Type **password cisco** and press **Enter**.

9. Type **exit** and press **Enter.** How far back does exit take you? _____

_____

10. Type **line aux 0** and press **Enter**. This tells the router that you want to configure the aux port. The prompt should change. For example, if the router name is lab-e, the prompt should change to lab-e(config-line)#.

11. Type **login** and press **Enter**.

12. Type **password cisco** and press **Enter**.

13. Press **Ctrl+Z.** How far back does this take you? _____

_____

14. Press **Enter** after you receive the message that the router has been configured by the console.

15. Type **show run** and press **Enter** to see the running configuration. Notice that the enable secret password is encrypted and looks nothing like the password, class, you entered during the System Configuration Dialog.

16. Press the **spacebar** to see more of the display.

17. Notice the console, aux, and virtual terminal password information. Are these passwords encrypted? _____

18. Type **copy run start** and press **Enter.** What does the copy run start command do? _____

_____

19. Is it really necessary to use this copy run start command, or are the configuration changes automatically saved? _____

_____

LAB 10.5 USE HELP, THE COMMAND HISTORY, ENHANCED EDITING FEATURES, AND THE SHOW COMMAND

10

Objective

The objective of this lab is to give you experience in getting command-line Help, using the Cisco enhanced editing features and command history, and using the very important show commands to determine information about your router. In this lab you will use Help and various show commands, and edit the command line using the editing features of the Cisco command executive. After completing this lab you will be able to:

➤ Get help on commands.

➤ Navigate the command line more efficiently.

➤ Understand the kinds of information you can obtain using the most popular show commands.

Materials Required

This lab requires:

➤ The Cisco Networking Academies Semester 2 Lab setup per Figure 10-2 and Lab 10.1

➤ Hyperterminal configured to access the routers via the console port per Lab 10.2

➤ The Cisco Networking Academies Semester 2 Lab configured per Lab 10.3 and Lab 10.4

ACTIVITY

1. Boot the computer into Windows 95/98, and begin the Hyperterminal session with the router.

2. Turn on the router if necessary. Press **Enter** to get the User Exec mode prompt, which should be the name of the router (for example, lab-e) and the greater than sign (>).

3. Type **?**. There is no need to press **Enter**. A list of commands should display. Press the **spacebar** to scroll through the list. What do these commands represent? _____

   _____

4. Type **show ?**. A list of commands should appear. What do these commands represent? _____

   _____

5. Type **show hosts** and press **Enter**. Does your router know about any other routers? Why or why not? _____

   _____

6. Type **show version** and press **Enter**. What is the name of the IOS image?

   _____

7. What version of the IOS is your router running? _____

   _____

8. Where did the system IOS boot from? _____

   _____

9. What is the configuration register setting, and where does this setting indicate the configuration file is loading from? _____

   _____

10. Type **ena** and press **Enter** to access Privileged Exec mode.

11. Type **class** and press **Enter** when prompted for the enable secret password. How did the prompt change? _____

    _____

12. Type **?**. Press the **spacebar** to scroll through the commands. What do these commands represent? _____

    _____

13. Type **show ?**. What do these commands represent? Why are there so many more commands in Privileged Exec mode than in User mode? ____

14. Use the **show flash** command to display information about the flash. What is the IOS filename? How big is the file? ____

15. Type **show int** and press **Enter**. What valuable information appears on the first line of the display? ____

16. What is the status of each interface on your router? ____

17. Which part of the interface status is associated with the physical layer, and which part is associated with the data-link layer? ____

18. Type **show prot** and press **Enter**. What protocol is enabled on your router? ____

19. What interface and address information appears? ____

10

20. Type **show arp** and press **Enter**. What information does this command display? ____

21. What do you think the command to clear the arp cache is? (Use Help to find out.) ____

22. Type **show start** and press **Enter**. What are you viewing the contents of?

23. What is the host name of the router? ____

24. What interfaces are available for configuration on the router? ____

25. What interfaces are actually configured on the router? ____

26. Is a routing protocol configured on the router? If so, what is it? ____

27. Type **sh ru** and press **Enter**. What are you viewing the contents of? ____

28. Is the running configuration supposed to be the same as the startup configuration? Explain. _____

_____

_____

_____

29. Type **sh hist** and press **Enter**. What appears? _____

_____

30. Press the **up arrow** until you see the show start command. What does the up arrow do? _____

31. Press **Ctrl+A**. What does this do? _____

32. Press **Ctrl+E**. What does this do? _____

33. Press **Esc+B**. What does this do? _____

34. Press **Esc+F**. What does this do? _____

35. Delete the word "start" by pressing the **backspace** key. Type **run** and press **Enter**.

36. When was the last time the show interface counters were cleared? _____

_____

37. Type **clear counters** and press **Enter**. What happens and when is this command valuable? _____

_____

_____

38. Press **Enter** to clear the message.

ROUTER STARTUP AND CONFIGURATION

LABS INCLUDED IN THIS CHAPTER

➤ Lab 11.1 Configure IP Addresses and IP Hosts

➤ Lab 11.2 Install and Configure a TFTP Server on the Internetwork

➤ Lab 11.3 Configure a Message and Interface Description

➤ Lab 11.4 Configure Static Routes, RIP, and IGRP

➤ Lab 11.5 CDP, Ping, Trace, and Telnet

➤ Lab 11.6 Troubleshooting Challenge

Lab 11.1 Configure IP Addresses and IP Hosts

Objective

The objective of this lab is to give you experience in configuring IP addresses without the aid of the System Configuration Dialog. In addition, you will make IP to host name mappings. IP to host name mappings can be configured using a name server or in this case, the router. In this lab you will use the IP address command to configure the router interfaces, and the IP host command to provide IP to host name mappings. After completing these commands and saving the configuration, the router will be completely configured per the Cisco Networking Academies Semester 2 Lab. After completing this lab you will be able to:

Configure IP to host name mappings using the IP host command.

Configure IP for each interface on the router.

Materials Required

This lab requires:

➤ The Cisco Networking Academies Semester 2 Lab setup

➤ Completion of all labs in Chapter 10, with the router configurations saved

Activity

Configure IP to Host Name Mappings

1. Boot the computer into Windows 95/98, and begin the Hyperterminal session with the router.

2. Turn on the router if necessary. Press **Enter** to start and type the password **cisco** to get to the User Exec mode prompt.

3. Type **ena** and press **Enter** to access Privileged Exec mode.

4. Type **class** and press **Enter** when prompted for the enable secret password.

5. Type **conf t** and press **Enter**. What is the name of this mode?

_____

6. Type **ip host**, the name of the first router in the lab, and all IP addresses associated with the interfaces on this first router. Then press **Enter**. This first router is typically named lab-a, so the command would be:

Ip host lab-a 192.5.5.1 205.7.5.1 201.100.11.1

The addresses in this example are the interfaces listed on the diagram of the network shown in Figure 11-1.

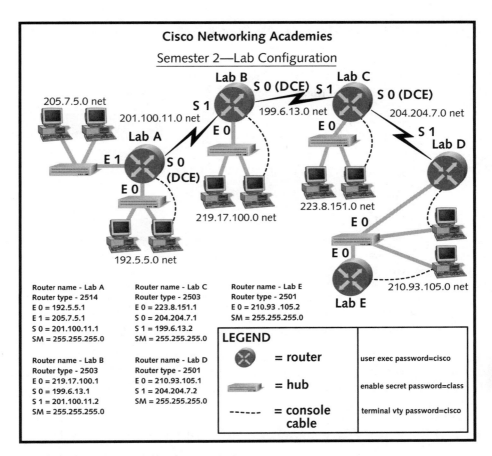

Figure 11-1   Standard network configuration

7. Repeat Step 6 for all routers. Each router will have the IP addresses of all routers in the internetwork.

8. Press **Ctrl+Z** to exit global configuration mode. Press **Enter** to clear the message.

9. What is the value of the IP host command? _____

_____

_____

10. Type **sh host** and press **Enter**. What hosts does your router know about?

_____

_____

_____

Configure Interface IP Addresses

11. Type **conf t** and press **Enter**.

12. Type **int e0** and press **Enter**. What mode are you in, and what will the next commands you type affect?

   _____

13. Configure the IP address of the Ethernet 0 interface, using the following as an example:

   Ip address 210.93.105.2 255.255.255.0

   No shutdown

14. What does the first line of the example in Step 13 represent?

   _____

   _____

15. What does the second line represent?

   _____

   _____

16. Type **exit** to return to global configuration mode.

17. Using Steps 12 and 13 as an example, configure the IP addresses of any additional interfaces that are to be configured per Figure 11-1. If you are configuring an S0 interface, make sure to add the line:

   Clock rate 56000

18. Why is this command necessary for the S0 interface? (HINT: DCE)

   _____

   _____

   _____

19. Press **Ctrl+Z** to return to the enable prompt.

20. Type **sh ru** to view the new running configuration. Check all commands and IP addresses, specifically the interfaces, router rip network numbers, and IP host addresses. If there are no mistakes, proceed to Step 25.

21. If there is a mistake in the interface configurations, return to Steps 11 through 20 and reconfigure the interfaces. Then go to Step 25.

22. If there is a mistake in the router rip, type **conf t** and press **Enter** to enter global configuration mode. Then type **no router rip** and press **Enter** to remove the incorrect rip information. If rip was not configured, you don't need to type the no router rip command. Now type **router rip** to enter router configuration mode. Enter the correct numbers of the networks that are attached to your router, using this command as an example:

   Network 210.93.105.0

23. Continue to use the network command until all networks attached to your router are listed. For example, the lab-a router will have three network command lines, because it is attached to three networks. Press **Ctrl+Z** to return to global configuration mode.

24. If there is no mistake in the list of IP hostnames, go to Step 25. If there is a mistake in the list of IP hostnames, type **conf t** and press **Enter**. Then type **no ip host** followed by the name of the router that has the error. Go to Steps 6 through 8, and reconfigure the IP to host name mappings.

25. If you are sure your running configuration is completely accurate, ask your instructor to evaluate it. When you are both sure it is correct, go to Step 26.

26. Type **copy run start** at the enable prompt to replace the start-up configuration file.

LAB 11.2 INSTALL AND CONFIGURE A TFTP SERVER ON THE INTERNETWORK

Objective

The objective of this lab is to show you the benefit of having a TFTP server on your network to configure the routers in the event they lose their IOS or configuration information. If you completed the labs in Chapter 10 and Lab 11.1 properly, your routers are configured to match the Cisco Networking Academies Semester 2 Lab setup. It is now appropriate to copy these configurations to a TFTP server. There is more than one kind of TFTP software. One of the easiest to use is Cisco's own TFTPServer.exe. In this lab you will add a computer to the Cisco Networking Academies Semester 2 Lab setup on the hub between routers lab-d and lab-e. This corresponds to network 210.93.105.0, as shown in Figure 10.2. You will then install and configure the TFTP server software. Next, you will copy the IOS and the router configuration files to the TFTP server. After completing this lab you will be able to:

➤ Install and configure TFTP server software.

➤ Copy the Cisco IOS from the router to the TFTP server.

➤ Copy router configurations to the TFTP server.

Materials Required

This lab requires:

➤ The Cisco Networking Academies Semester 2 Lab setup

➤ Completion of all labs in Chapter 10

➤ Completion of Lab 11.1, with the router configurations saved

11

➤ A Windows 95/98 computer with a NIC configured and the TCP/IP protocol configured

➤ UTP patch cable

➤ TFTP server software

Activity

Configuring the TFTP Server

1. Place the TFTP server in close proximity to the computer attached to the lab-e router, as shown in Figure 11-1.

2. Attach one end of the UTP patch cable to the NIC on the TFTP server.

3. Attach the other end of the UTP patch cable to the hub between router lab-d and router lab-e, as shown in Figure 11-1.

4. Turn on the computer and let it boot into Windows 95/98.

5. Put the diskette with the TFTP server software on it in drive A of the TFTP server.

6. Click **Start** and then click **Run**.

7. Click the **Browse** button to search for an executable on drive A. Double-click the executable to install the TFTP server software.

8. Right-click **Network Neighborhood** and click **Properties**.

9. Click the **Configuration** tab if necessary.

10. Double-click **TCP/IP**.

11. Give the TFTP server an IP address on the network that it is attached to. If the server patch cable has been attached to the hub between router lab-d and router lab-e, the network is 210.93.105.0, as shown in Figure 11-1. This figure shows that the E0 interfaces on routers lab-d and lab-e are using 210.93.105.1 and 210.93.105.2. Using this example, the next available host number for the TFTP server is 210.93.105.3.

12. What IP address did you give the TFTP server?

_____

13. You also need to provide the subnet mask for the TFTP server. It should be the same as the network to which it is attached, in this example, 255.255.255.0.

14. Click the **Gateway** tab. A gateway must be configured on the network hosts so that they can get out to the internetwork. Typically, the gateway is the serial interface on the router that leads to the rest of the internetwork. In this example, the gateway is 204.204.7.2, which is the serial interface on the lab-d router, as shown in Figure 11-1. Type this **IP address** and click the **Add** button.

15. Click **OK** twice to close the Network Dialog box. You will be prompted to restart the computer. Make sure there is no diskette in Drive a:. Click **Yes** to restart.

16. After the computer restarts, open the TFTP program by clicking **Start,** clicking **Programs**, and then clicking the name of the TP program; or by double-clicking a desktop shortcut if one exists.

Backing Up the Configuration File

1. Move to a router terminal, and boot the computer into Windows 95/98 if necessary.

2. Begin the Hyperterminal session with a router.

3. Turn on the router if necessary. Press **Enter** to start and then type **cisco** for the User Exec mode password.

4. Type **ena** and press **Enter** to access Privileged Exec mode.

5. Type **class** and press **Enter** when prompted for the enable secret password.

6. What command will you type to look at the active configuration?

_____

7. Use the command you recorded in the Step 6, and double check to make sure it has been configured correctly per Figure 11-1.

8. Begin by pinging the TFTP server to make sure you have connectivity. Type **ping** followed by the IP address you configured on the TFTP server and recorded in Step 12 above. If your ping fails, you should check all connections and the TCP/IP configuration on the TFTP server. When you can ping the TFTP server successfully, proceed to Step 9.

9. Type **copy run tftp** and press **Enter** to begin the process of backing up the running configuration to the TFTP server. This command fails if the TFTP server software is not running.

10. Next you are prompted for the IP address of the TFTP server. Type the IP address you recorded in Step 12 above, and press **Enter**.

11. You are prompted for the name of the configuration file. The default, which is indicated in square brackets, is the router name followed by a hyphen and then "confg." For example, the lab-e configuration file will be named lab-e-confg. Press **Enter** to accept the default.

12. Press **Enter** again to confirm.

11

Backing Up the IOS

1. Type **show flash** and press **Enter**. What is the name of the IOS image of the router? _____

2. Type **copy flash tftp** to begin the process of backing up the router operating system (IOS) on the TFTP server.

3. Once again, you are prompted for the IP address of the TFTP server. Type the IP address you recorded in Step 12 above, and press **Enter**.

4. You are prompted for the source filename. Type the name of the file you recorded in Step 1.

5. Next you are prompted for the destination filename. The default (indicated in square brackets) is the same name you typed for the source filename in Step 4. Press **Enter** to accept the default.

6. After the verification process, the router asks you to confirm the copy. Type **Y** and press **Enter** to confirm.

7. The back-up process usually takes 20 to 30 minutes.

8. Go back to the TFTP server, and search for the backed-up files. When the router lab is completely backed up, you should have five configuration files and one IOS file on the TFTP server. Your routers may have different versions of the IOS on them. In this case, you should have one backup for each version.

LAB 11.3 CONFIGURE A MESSAGE AND INTERFACE DESCRIPTION

Objective

The objective of this lab is to show you how to customize your router further by configuring a message of the day and by assigning descriptions to interfaces. In this lab you will use the banner motd command and the description command to customize your router. After completing this lab you will be able to:

➤ Use the banner motd command to provide a message for anyone accessing the router.

➤ Use the description command to add information to a configured interface.

Materials Required

This lab requires:

➤ The Cisco Networking Academies Semester 2 Lab setup

➤ Completion of all labs in Chapter 10, as well as Lab 11.1

Activity

Banner Motd

1. Boot the computer into Windows 95/98, and begin the Hyperterminal session with the router.

2. Turn on the router if necessary. Press **Enter** to start and type the password **cisco** to get to the User Exec mode prompt.

3. Type **ena** and press **Enter** to access Privileged Exec mode.

4. Type **class** and press **Enter** when prompted for the enable secret password.

5. Type **conf t** and press **Enter** to enter global configuration mode.

6. Type **banner motd #** and press **Enter**. What message appears?

   _____

   _____

7. Type **Welcome to the Cisco Series 2500 router**.

8. Type **#** and press **Enter** to signal the end of your message.

9. Press Ctrl + Z to exit Global Configuration mode.

10. Type **reload** and press **Enter**.

11. Press **Enter** to start. Do you see the message of the day?

    _____

12. Enter the password **cisco** to get to the User Exec mode prompt.

13. Type **ena** and press **Enter** to access Privileged Exec mode.

14. Type **class** and press **Enter** when prompted for the enable secret password.

15. Type **conf t** and press **Enter** to enter global configuration mode.

16. Type **no banner motd #** and press **Enter**. This removes the message of the day.

Description Command

1. From the global configuration mode prompt, type **int e0** to enter interface configuration mode. What does the prompt change to?

   _____

2. Type **description Attached to Ethernet LAN lab-e** (substitute the name of your router if necessary) and press **Enter**.

3. Press **Ctrl+Z** to return to the enable prompt.

11

4. Type **show interfaces**. Does the description configured for e0 appear?

_____

5. Type **logout** to exit the router.

LAB 11.4 CONFIGURE STATIC ROUTES, RIP, AND IGRP

Objective

The two components necessary to make a router operational are the configuration of the interfaces and a method of finding routes to other routers. Two methods used for finding routes are to let the routers update each other through dynamic routing protocols or to statically configure the routes using the IP route command. The objective of this lab is to show you how to configure the router using both methods. In this lab you will configure the router for the RIP and IGRP dynamic routing protocols. Then you will use the IP route command to configure static routes. It is also important to memorize the output provided by the show protocols and show IP route commands. After completing this lab you will:

➤ Understand the difference between dynamic routing and static routing.

➤ Understand the command syntax for configuring dynamic and static routing.

➤ Know how to check the router for routing table information.

➤ Be familiar with the output from the show protocols and show IP route commands.

Materials Required

This lab requires:

➤ The Cisco Networking Academies Semester 2 Lab setup

➤ Completion of all labs in Chapter 10, as well as Lab 11.1

Activity

Getting Routing Information

1. Boot the computer into Windows 95/98, and begin the Hyperterminal session with the router.

2. Turn on the router if necessary. Press **Enter** to start and type the password **cisco** to get to the User Exec mode prompt.

3. Type **ena** and press **Enter** to access Privileged Exec mode.

4. Type **class** and press **Enter** when prompted for the enable secret password.

5. Type **show ip route** and press **Enter** to see the routing table information on the router.

6. What networks directly connect to your router? How do you know if a network is directly connected? _____

_____

7. Has your router learned about any networks through the rip routing protocol? How do you know if your router has learned about a network through rip? _____

_____

8. Has your router learned about any networks through static configuration? How do you know if a route to a network has been statically configured?

_____

_____

9. Type **debug IP rip** and press **Enter**. Watch the screen for a minute or so to see the displayed information. How is this command useful? Can you think of any problems associated with leaving this command activated?

_____

_____

_____

10. Type **no debug** and press **Enter** to disable debugging.

11. Type **conf t** and press **Enter** to enter global configuration mode.

Configuring the IGRP Routing Protocol

1. Type **no router rip** to disable the rip routing protocol that was configured during the System Configuration Dialog in Chapter 10.

2. You should still be in global configuration mode. Type **router igrp 100** and press **Enter** to enter router configuration mode. What did the prompt change to? What does the number 100 represent? _____

_____

3. Use the **network** command to indicate which networks are directly connected to your router. For example, if your router is connected to networks 204.204.7.0 and 210.93.105.0, you type:

network 204.204.7.0 and press **Enter**

network 210.93.105.0 and press **Enter**

4. Press **Ctrl+Z** to return to the enable prompt. Press **Enter** to clear the message.

5. Type **show ip prot** and press **Enter**. Is RIP configured on the router? _____ Is IGRP configured on the router? _____

6. Type **debug ip igrp transactions** and press **Enter**. Watch the screen for a minute or so to see the displayed information. What useful information can be obtained from this command?

_____

_____

7. Type **no debug ip igrp transactions** and press **Enter** to disable debugging.

8. Type **conf t** and press **Enter** to enter global configuration mode.

Configuring the RIP Routing Protocol

9. Type **router rip** to enter router configuration mode.

10. Use the **network** command to indicate which networks are directly connected to your router. For example, if your router is connected to networks 204.204.7.0 and 210.93.105.0, you type:

    network 204.204.7.0 and press **Enter**

    network 210.93.105.0 and press **Enter**

11. Press **Ctrl+Z** to return to the enable prompt. Press **Enter** to clear the message.

12. Type **show ip route** and press **[Enter]**. What networks does your router know about and how has your router obtained this information?

_____

_____

_____

Configuring Static Routes

1. To configure a static route on a router, you must know the destination network number, the subnet mask, and the IP address of the next router interface (hop) in the path to the destination network. For example, if you are configuring the Lab E router in the Cisco Semester 2 Lab shown in Figure 10.2, and you want to configure a static route to network 205.7.5.0, you type:

    Ip route 205.7.5.0 255.255.255.0 210.93.105.1

    The last IP address in the command is the Eo interface on the Lab D router and corresponds to the next hop on the path to the destination network.

2. Type **conf t** and press **Enter** to enter global configuration mode.

3. Use the **ip route** command to configure a static route on your router. Which router are you configuring?

_____

4. For which router are you configuring a static route?

_____

5. What command did you enter?

_____

6. Press **Ctrl+Z** to return to the enable prompt. Press **Enter** to clear the message.

7. Type **show ip route** and press **Enter** to see the routing table information on the router.

8. Which networks are directly connected to your router? How do you know? _____

_____

9. Is any routing information being obtained from dynamic routing protocols? If yes, what are the network numbers and how are they obtained?

_____

10. Has your router learned about any networks through the static configuration? If yes, what are the network numbers?

_____

11. Do routing protocols know anything about specific hosts on a network? How do you know? _____

_____

_____

12. Type **conf t** and press **Enter** to enter global configuration mode.

13. Type **no router igrp 100** and press **Enter** to remove the IGRP routing protocol from your router.

14. Type **logout** and press **Enter** to exit the router.

LAB 11.5 CDP, PING, TRACE, AND TELNET

Objective

The Cisco Discovery Protocol (CDP) shares configuration information between locally connected Cisco devices. The various show CDP commands tell you about routers and switches that are directly connected to your router. The ping and trace commands provide connectivity information at the network layer of the OSI reference model and are used primarily for troubleshooting. The telnet application provides application layer connectivity information and lets you access remote routers. The objective of this lab is to familiarize you with the displayed output of the various show CDP commands. In addition, you should become very familiar with the ping, trace, and telnet commands, because they are the most frequently used network troubleshooting tools. After completing this lab you will:

➤ Be familiar with the output generated by the various CDP commands.

➤ Understand how to test for network layer connectivity using the ping and trace commands.

➤ Know how to use the telnet application to access routers remotely.

Materials Required

This lab requires:

➤ The Cisco Networking Academies Semester 2 Lab setup

➤ Completion of all labs in Chapter 10, as well as Lab 11.1

Activity

Using the Show CDP Commands

1. Boot the computer into Windows 95/98, and begin the Hyperterminal session with the router.

2. Turn on the router if necessary. Press **Enter** to start and type the password **cisco** to get to the User Exec mode prompt.

3. Type **ena** and press **Enter** to access Privileged Exec mode.

4. Type **class** and press **Enter** when prompted for the enable secret password.

5. Type **show cdp neigh** and press **Enter** to get information regarding the directly connected neighbors. Who is one of your neighbors? What local interface are they on? What kind of device is it? What other information does this show command provide?

_____

_____

6. Press **up arrow** until you get to the show CDP neigh command. Press **Ctrl+E** to move to the end of the command, type **det,** and press **Enter**. What additional information do you get when you add "details" to the show cdp neighbors command?

_____

_____

7. Type **show cdp interface** and press **Enter**. What is the fundamental difference between the output of this command and the output of the show cdp neigh commands? _____

_____

_____

Using Ping and Trace

1. Type **ping** and then type an IP address of a remote router interface. For example, if you are on the Lab B router and want to check for connectivity to the Lab D, S1 interface, you type:

   Ping 204.204.7.2 and press **Enter**

2. Was the ping successful? _____ What symbol indicates a successful ping? _____ What other symbols might you see in a ping response, and what do they mean? _____

   _____

   If your ping succeeded, what were the minimum, average, and maximum roundtrip times?

   _____

3. Type **ping** and press **Enter**. How does the extended mode ping command respond? What does this imply? _____

   _____

   _____

4. Press **Enter** to accept the default protocol. Enter any remote IP address. Change the repeat count to **20**. Change the datagram size to **1500**. Continue to press **Enter** to accept the defaults for the remaining prompts. How does this output differ from the output from the ping command you issued in Step 1? _____

   _____

5. Type **trace** and then type the IP address of an interface on the farthest remote router from your location. For example, if you are on the Lab B router and want to check for connectivity to the Lab E, Eo interface, you type:

   Trace 210.93.105.2 and press **Enter**

6. Was the trace successful? What information is obtained from the trace command? What is the advantage of using the trace command instead of the ping command? _____

   _____

   _____

7. At which layer of the OSI reference model do ping and trace operate?

   _____

8. At which layer of the TCP/IP reference model do ping and trace operate?

   _____

11

Telnet

1. Type **telnet** and then type the IP address of an interface on a remote router. For example, if you are on the Lab B router and want to telnet to the Lab E router, you type:

   Telnet 210.93.105.2 and press **Enter**

   Alternatively, you could use the name of the router to which you would like to connect. For example, you could type:

   Telnet lab–e and press **Enter**

2. What makes it possible to use names with the telnet application? (HINT: See Lab 11.1.) _____

3. Did the telnet succeed? _____

4. If the telnet failed, try telnetting to a different router until you can telnet successfully. Ask your instructor for help if necessary.

5. You should be prompted for a password when you telnet successfully. Type **cisco** and press **Enter**. Is this the same kind of password you are prompted for when you log on to a router locally? _____ Exactly what kind of password is this? _____

   _____

6. Type **ena** and press **Enter** to access Privileged Exec mode.

7. Type **class** and press **Enter** when prompted for the enable secret password.

8. Type **sh ru** and press **Enter**. Exactly what do you see?

   _____

9. Type **show cdp neigh det** and press **Enter**. What is the advantage of using the telnet application in conjunction with the show cdp neigh commands?

   _____

   _____

10. At which layer of the OSI reference model is telnet operating?

    _____

11. At which layer of the TCP/IP reference model is telnet operating?

    _____

12. As a troubleshooting tool, what advantages does telnet have over ping and trace? _____

    _____

13. Type **logout** and press **Enter** to terminate your telnet session.

14. Type **logout** and press **Enter** to exit the router.

LAB 11.6 TROUBLESHOOTING CHALLENGE

Objective

The objective of this lab is to teach you how to troubleshoot common router connectivity and configuration problems. In this lab, you and a team of other students will work together to solve problems your instructor intentionally introduced to the Cisco Networking Academies Semester 2 Lab. You should attempt to identify the problems and understand which layer the problems are associated with. When you finish, the Cisco Networking Academies Semester 2 Lab should function as it is designed to do. After completing this lab you will:

➤ Be familiar with common troubleshooting techniques.

➤ Understand at which layers common problems occur.

➤ Be familiar with the show commands most useful in troubleshooting.

Materials Required

This lab requires:

➤ The Cisco Networking Academies Semester 2 Lab setup

➤ Completion of all labs in Chapter 10, as well as Lab 11.1

➤ Simple cable tester

➤ RJ-45 connectors

➤ Cat 5 UTP cable

➤ Wire cutters and crimpers

➤ Paper and pencil to record troubleshooting information

Activity

Troubleshooting Steps

1. Begin at the Lab A router. Ping the TFTP server. Does it work?

   _____

2. Use the trace command to trace to the TFTP server. Where is the problem?

   _____

3. On which router will you begin troubleshooting? Why? _____

   _____

4. Log on to the router on which you would like to begin troubleshooting.

5. Which show command gives you information regarding the status of the interfaces on the router?

   _____

6. Use the show command you recorded in Step 5 to check the router. List the interfaces and their status. Which part of the output relates to the physical layer, and which part of the output relates to the data-link layer?

_____

_____

7. How do you interpret the output of Step 6? _____

_____

_____

8. Use the same command you used in Step 5 on each router to get interface information. Have you discovered any physical layer problems with the lab? _____ Which router interfaces have a physical layer problem?

_____

_____

_____

9. Make sure all devices are turned on. Check all cables to make sure they are correctly connected. Did you find any devices that were not turned on? _____ Did you find any cables that were not correctly connected? _____ If yes, which cables had a problem?

_____

_____

_____

10. Repeat Step 8 to see if the physical problems have been corrected. Are there any data-link layer problems? _____ If yes, where and what do you think could be the cause?

_____

_____

_____

11. Are the DCE and DTE cable ends matched to the appropriate serial interfaces? _____ Is the clock rate set for the DCE ends? _____ After these problems have been corrected, attempt to ping the TFTP server from the Lab A router again. Does it work?

_____

12. Try the trace command from the Lab A router to the TFTP server. Does it work? _____ Where is the problem?

_____

13. Move to the TFTP server. Open a DOS window and attempt to ping the Lab D router. Did it work? _____

14. Use the simple cable tester to test the patch cable between the TFTP server and the hub. If there is a problem with the patch cable, what is it?

_____

15. Fix the problem you detected in Step 14 if necessary. With which layer are cable problems associated? _____

16. Attempt to ping the Lab A router from the TFTP server again. If it doesn't work, check the network configuration for the TFTP server. Make sure the IP and gateway information is correct.

17. Which show command can you use to determine how the routers are being updated with routing table information? Check each router for routing protocol information using this command. Do you see any problems? _____ If yes, what are they? _____

_____

18. Reconfigure any routers for the appropriate routing protocols. With which layer are routing protocol problems associated? _____

_____

19. Move to the Lab A router, and use the **telnet 210.93.105.2** command to attempt a session with the Lab E router. Did it work? _____ At which layer is the telnet application operating? _____

_____

11

20. Log out of the Lab E router.

21. Now try telnetting to the Lab E router again using the **telnet lab–e** command. Did it work? _____ What could be the problem with using a name rather than an IP address with the telnet command?

_____

_____ Which show command can you use to make sure the router has a host name to IP address mapping table?

_____

22. Use the appropriate show command on each router to check for the host name table. Reconfigure any router if necessary. Then, attempt to telnet to a router using the host name instead of the IP address.

23. Log out of any telnet session. Log out of the local routers. Ask your instructor to check your Cisco Networking Academies Semester 2 Lab setup.